BITS AND PIECES

TWO PLAYS
BREAKFAST, LUNCH, AND DINNER
&
BITS AND PIECES
BY CORINNE JACKER

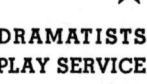
DRAMATISTS
PLAY SERVICE
INC.

BITS AND PIECES
Copyright © 1975, Corinne Jacker

All Rights Reserved

CAUTION: Professionals and amateurs are hereby warned that the Plays in the volume BITS AND PIECES are subject to a royalty. The Plays are fully protected under the copyright laws of the United States of America, and of all countries covered by the International Copyright Union (including the Dominion of Canada and the rest of the British Commonwealth), and of all countries covered by the Pan-American Copyright Convention, the Universal Copyright Convention, the Berne Convention, and of all countries with which the United States has reciprocal copyright relations. All rights, including professional/amateur stage rights, motion picture, recitation, lecturing, public reading, radio broadcasting, television, video or sound recording, all other forms of mechanical or electronic reproduction, such as CD-ROM, CD-I, DVD, information storage and retrieval systems and photocopying, and the rights of translation into foreign languages, are strictly reserved. Particular emphasis is placed upon the matter of readings, permission for which must be secured from the Author's agent in writing.

The non-professional stage performance rights in the Plays in the volume BITS AND PIECES are controlled exclusively by DRAMATISTS PLAY SERVICE, INC., 440 Park Avenue South, New York, NY 10016. No non-professional performance of either Play may be given without obtaining in advance the written permission of DRAMATISTS PLAY SERVICE, INC., and paying the requisite fee.

Inquiries concerning all other rights should be addressed to Berman, Boals and Flynn, 208 West 30th Street, Suite 401, New York, NY 10001.

SPECIAL NOTE

Anyone receiving permission to produce any or all of the Plays in BITS AND PIECES is required to give credit to the Author as sole and exclusive Author of the Play(s) on the title page of all programs distributed in connection with performances of the Play(s) and in all instances in which the title(s) of the Play(s) appears for purposes of advertising, publicizing or otherwise exploiting the Play(s) and/or a production thereof. The name of the Author must appear on a separate line, in which no other name appears, immediately beneath the title(s) and in size of type equal to 50% of the size of the largest, most prominent letter used for the title(s) the Play(s). No person, firm or entity may receive credit larger or more prominent than that accorded the Author.

BREAKFAST, LUNCH, AND DINNER

The first professional production of BREAKFAST, LUNCH, AND DINNER was in New York City at the Actors' Studio, in May, 1972, with the following cast:

(in order of appearance)

BARBARA .... Margaret Linn

RICHARD .... Sam Schacht

EMILY .... Kay Michaels

Directed by Kim Friedman

BREAKFAST, LUNCH, AND DINNER

Scene 1. BREAKFAST

The large kitchen of Richard and Barbara's home. It is an old house, located on an acre of land in Westchester. The floors are tile, the walls are wood, and a few years ago Richard bought some old beams from a farm that was being torn down and they are up on the ceiling. The stove, refrigerator-freezer, etc., are all copper finished. But the whole effect is somehow very personal, definitely not House and Garden. There are doors and archways that lead to the bedrooms, the living room, and one door leads to the outside. The kitchen was originally designed to be the heart of the house, and Barbara has done nothing to change that. There is a fireplace.
Richard is reading the New York Times. Barbara is drying some dishes she has just finished washing. There are a lot, they were left over from a very elaborate supper, followed by heavy drinking and snacks. When she finishes that, she will set the table, put out glasses, squeeze orange juice. She is always busy, never still.

BARBARA. I was just thinking of Stephen Spender . . . You know that wonderful line of his: "I think continually of those who were truly great" . . . Or—wait—is it "on those who were truly great?" . . . I can't remember what comes next. We don't own any Spender, do we? (*Silence. Richard hasn't responded at all. He is aggressively reading the paper. Barbara's tone suddenly changes.*) Is this a confrontation between us?
RICHARD. There's trouble in the Mideast again.
BARBARA. Make breakfast then.
RICHARD. The stock market fell ten points.
BARBARA. Make pancakes.
RICHARD. It's your sister who's come here for the weekend, not mine.
BARBARA. You don't have a sister.

RICHARD. If I did, you wouldn't like her.
BARBARA. What will it take to get you out of your mood?
RICHARD. I'm not in a mood. (*Pause.*) Why do you want a confrontation?
BARBARA. I don't want one. I merely asked if this was one.
RICHARD. One what about what?
BARBARA. Anything . . . I don't care. Read your paper.
RICHARD. Would you be happier if I read the editorials? (*No one talks. After a moment, he looks at his watch.*) She's a late sleeper, isn't she?
BARBARA. Emily? Do you resent that? (*No answer.*) All right. Let's talk. Emily says it's better to ventilate the emotions.
RICHARD. Like musty attics?
BARBARA. Isn't that metaphor a little petty? (*Pause.*)
RICHARD. I offered to cook because I like to cook.
BARBARA. No one wants to stifle anyone's creativity. You know where everything is.
RICHARD. You think you own this kitchen.
BARBARA. Are we re-evaluating our relationship?
RICHARD. Where's the pancake mix?
BARBARA. (*After a moment.*) We don't even read the same books any more.
RICHARD. You and I have different interests. I'm a man.
BARBARA. What's that got to do with anything?
RICHARD. All right! What do you want out of life?
BARBARA. Because I said it was a good thing we didn't have children?
RICHARD. You're always saying that.
BARBARA. Children justify a woman's existence. They need mothers. There was a study about monkeys and a vinyl mother. They fed them all milk. But one group was fed by the real, animal mother and the others were fed by this vinyl machine. And the ones that were fed by the dummy grew up crazy. What do you think of that?
RICHARD. Children don't like me.
BARBARA. Because you treat them like potential clients.
RICHARD. You can't get along without challenging the most basic realities of my existence, can you?
BARBARA. Do you sleep with other women? (*He looks at her.*) I'm curious.

RICHARD. How far do you want this argument to go?
BARBARA. Please, I don't want to argue.
RICHARD. You started it.
BARBARA. My sister is here for the weekend. Things should be pleasant. Relaxed. (*Pause.*) I do yoga exercises every day. See, how limber my body is. (*She demonstrates a difficult-looking posture.*) Do you think that means that I have peace of mind?
RICHARD. We happen to live in violent and savage times.
BARBARA. This is a marriage in which no one ever speaks seriously.
RICHARD. I get tired at night. So I spend my free time reading mysteries or *Playboy* instead of The Making of the Counter Culture. I *am* the god-damned culture they want to counter. And I haven't tried to write for a number of years. That's true.
BARBARA. How long has it been since you were at a museum?
RICHARD. Some time, I'd like to see you earn a living for this family.
BARBARA. Even if I were an accountant I'd earn less money. I bet your firm pays women less then men. Doesn't it?
RICHARD. I'm not an administrator.
BARBARA. Oh, you are so conniving. I suppose that's what comes of an immoral profession.
RICHARD. There are loopholes written into our tax laws. I just try to do well by my clients. The government expects it of us.
BARBARA. Then why don't accountants work for the poor?
RICHARD. They don't need it.
BARBARA. When Emily worked for Radio Free Europe, we didn't talk to one another for two years. She wrote scripts for them during the Hungarian Revolution. (*Pause. Richard opens the paper and starts the crossword puzzle. Barbara is busy in the kitchen. She decides to heat the coffee.*)
RICHARD. I'll start on the pancakes.
BARBARA. One would assume she's on a diet.
RICHARD. You're not.
BARBARA. I happen to have a special metabolism. Emily always tended to fat. (*At the moment she is speaking, Emily comes in. She is two years older than her sister. She has just finished a shower and is wrapped only in a towel.*)
EMILY. Hi. I thought I heard signs of life . . . You know what I feel like? Pancakes. Lots of them. Thin, small and hot—right off the griddle.

BARBARA. Aren't your feet cold?
EMILY. You know what mother used to say. If you haven't seen it, you won't recognize it, and if you have, it won't thrill you. (*Richard smiles.*) I don't like to wear clothes—unless I have to.
BARBARA. You have to here.
EMILY. Why? I like being honest. When I have roommates they don't mind. Some of them like it.
RICHARD. I'll have breakfast ready by the time you're dressed.
BARBARA. You're dripping water all over my floor.
EMILY. You're a very special person, Richard. (*She goes out.*)
RICHARD. You're jealous of her.
BARBARA. Who?
RICHARD. Sibling rivalry.
BARBARA. Oh, shit.
RICHARD. That's why you drank so much last night.
BARBARA. Oh, my . . . None are so blind as those that will not see.
RICHARD. Why is she here?
BARBARA. I'd like to live ruled only by my instincts. Like an aborigine. (*Richard has started to assemble the makings of the batter. Now he comes over to her, takes her in his arms and kisses her.*)
RICHARD. Let's not fight. Come on, honey. Come on, look at me. Next weekend, let's go to Maine. Some island where there's a lot of natural wildlife.
BARBARA. (*After a moment.*) Maybe.
RICHARD. (*Turned off.*) Afraid you'd miss a meeting?
BARBARA. I'm sorry. There have been things on my mind.
RICHARD. You could talk them over with Emily.
BARBARA. What does she know about me?
RICHARD. She's your sister.
BARBARA. Exactly.
EMILY. (*Comes back, now she is in a robe. She goes over to Barbara and kisses her lightly on the cheek.*) We've never found it easy to talk to one another, Dick. Maybe we're too close in age. Like twins.
BARBARA. You've changed.
EMILY. Yes. (*She goes over and kisses Richard on the back of his neck.*) Are you a good cook?
RICHARD. Inspired.

EMILY. All the best chefs the world has produced have been men.
BARBARA. Where are you going? When you leave here?
EMILY. What an odd question.
BARBARA. Why?
EMILY. I don't know. You thrust it into the conversation. You know how much honesty matters to me. But you always were like that. Change the subject, interrupt like a dog, you have to go right to it. It used to drive me crazy.
BARBARA. I know.
EMILY. Oh you do?
BARBARA. What does that mean?
EMILY. Nothing . . . I'm going back to my apartment.
BARBARA. You told me you were going to sublet it.
EMILY. I worry a lot about identity. I was. Now I'm not.
RICHARD. All right. Here we are. The first two pancakes. Ready? (*And he brings two pancakes precariously balanced on a spatula.*)
EMILY. Anything I can do to help?
RICHARD. I like to do it myself. It's an obsession.
EMILY. I lived with an accountant. For a few months. In Washington. He was completely obsessive. He always washed his hands: before eating, or sex, or reading—even when he was going to watch tv . . . He had terrible dry skin problems.
RICHARD. I didn't mean like that.
EMILY. (*To Richard.*) Have you ever tried writing about your analysis?
RICHARD. Who told you I was in analysis.
EMILY. I just assumed . . . It's a core problem we all have.
RICHARD. I don't write any more.
EMILY. Oh.
RICHARD. That was a pretty meaningful oh.
EMILY. Well, some things become apparent. You're too aggressive, too hostile, too sensitive about your virility not to be a writer. It takes one to know one.
BARBARA. (*To Emily.*) Oh. Do you have a virility problem?
EMILY. You discourage him, of course. You never approved of writers.
BARBARA. Richard is tired at night. He spends his time reading mysteries and *Playboy*.
EMILY. I understand! We're sisters. I'm a famous writer. When you married him, he could have been a substitute for me. Is he?

BARBARA. No . . . You weren't famous then.
RICHARD. I was an only child.
BARBARA. (*Touches Emily with affection.*) Eat your pancakes.
RICHARD. (*Taking the plate away from Emily.*) They're cold now. I'll make fresh ones. (*Emily smiles at Richard, reaches into her robe pocket and takes out a small packet of cigars. Takes one out and lights it.*)
BARBARA. Come to the meeting with me. Both of you.
RICHARD. Forget it.
BARBARA. (*Smiles with difficulty. To Emily.*) My husband has no social conscience.
RICHARD. One of those in any family's enough. (*Pause.*)
EMILY. What you two both need is a chance to ventilate. A good encounter session. A marathon weekend. You'd reach a whole new reality level. I was at a marathon weekend last month. With a friend. And there was a man. I hated him on sight. He had terrible breath. He wore plastic rimmed glasses—the clear ones—and I knew I was going to explode before the weekend was over. I did. About midnight of the second night he was asking my friend something. And I smelled his breath . . . I went into a rage. I hit him, I scratched his cheek with my nails, I tried to knee him in the groin. And then I cried. For a long time.
RICHARD. I'm sorry.
EMILY. No. It released a deep fear of instability in me. We're working on it in my private sessions now. The doctor thinks I've hit a whole new level of awareness. If I hadn't gone, if I hadn't been open to releasing my aggressions, it could have been months, years before I made the same discovery.
BARBARA. This is interesting. This is organic. I've been listening to the three of us. And I'm shocked we are only able to talk about ourselves. We don't talk about the news, or the president. Or the army. Or the crime rate, how many rapes and murders there've been, pollution, any of that. That's cocktail talk, when we're not serious. But Emily is trying to be basic and sincere and reveal herself. And what does she talk about? How much bad breath annoys her. It's shameful. We should be working. We should be up in the morning and in Harlem or the Barrio, talking with people, trying to help them. Dick should be in the country, planting trees. Do you know what a problem reforestation is starting to be? Western civilization is disintegrating all around us, and we're sitting having

pancakes and coffee and being self-indulgent. The only reality should be work, commitment. Yes. If I could sit down with one little black boy, one Puerto Rican child and enroll him in our world, I'd have done something. (*During Barbara's talk, Emily and Richard have felt more drawn to one another, more interested in what each had indicated to the other. Richard gets up, pours Barbara coffee. Emily reaches her hand out to him. He takes it. She indicates her empty cup. He pours her a cup.*)
EMILY. That's very estimable.
BARBARA. I'm going to get dressed. Don't anybody go anywhere. (*She goes to the bedroom.*)
EMILY. (*To Richard.*) I do serious writing, too.
RICHARD. (*Pause.*) Our marriage rests on a good foundation, Emily.
EMILY. What's wrong?
RICHARD. (*Hesitation.*) I am writing. I just don't tell her. I'm working on a play . . . It's about something crucial that happened to me when I was a boy.
EMILY. What sign were you born under?
RICHARD. Aries.
EMILY. I thought so.
RICHARD. What does that mean?
EMILY. And Barbara's Leo . . . Not a typical one.
RICHARD. Is that what's wrong?
EMILY. I believe in astrology. I've tried a little white magic. Drawn a couple of pentagrams. For a while, I was friendly with some warlocks and witches. I went as an observer to their coven. But they had no sense of their own identity.
RICHARD. That's a little far out for me.
EMILY. I wouldn't expect a man to be interested. I don't like men much. Except in bed.
RICHARD. Well, I feel the same way about women.
EMILY. No you don't. (*Short pause.*) I tried to kill myself last week. Barbara didn't want me to be alone. That's why I'm here.
RICHARD. I didn't know—what about your doctor?
EMILY. I haven't told him. Do you want to know why?
RICHARD. She should have told me.
EMILY. I'll tell you some time.
RICHARD. How about another cup of coffee?
EMILY. What's your play about?

RICHARD. We'll talk about it some other time.
EMILY. Come on. You're dying to tell somebody.
RICHARD. It's still very rough. But the actual incident happened when I was a boy. We used to go to a lake in Canada for the summer. We were the only people for miles around. And we lived in a cabin. Right on the water. And I'd pretend I owned the lake. And I could swim naked in it if I wanted to. Anything.
EMILY. And you enjoyed it.
RICHARD. No. I just liked the fishing. That lake was full of them—trout, big mouth bass, pike. Almost every day I went out in the boat, I came home with four or five . . . Well we had this rainy spell, and I had to stay inside. I was just getting over a cold and my mother didn't want to take any chances. She even had a fight about it with my father . . . I was just sulking around. So finally I decided to do something about it. I got out of the house and went down to the shore. The trout were jumping. But the fishing wouldn't have been any good. It never is in the middle of a rain . . . I remember there was a dark gray sky. And the sun was just coming through in a couple of places so that you could see the rays, like in those pictures of the Resurrection. I got my rod and cast out into the lake. But I didn't bait the hook. Deliberately. I decided I was going to test Christ—set up a confrontation. If he really existed, one of the fish would grab onto my bare hook. It happens. It wouldn't be any kind of a miracle, I was just asking for the highly improbable. Well, I cast and cast. Then my father came yelling out of the house. He made me come inside, and in all the confusion my pole got left out. It was all rusty by the time I was out of bed again. My mother wouldn't even talk to me. She rubbed my chest with a mustard plaster and put *Vicks Vaporub* all over my nose and neck and made me drink hot milk. I didn't get very sick—just a normal kind of cold. But the weather stayed damp and I couldn't go out for a while. And that first night, I dreamt of Jesus—I don't remember the dream, only that I sweated a lot. When I woke up in the morning I had a gigantic hickey on the side of my nose.
EMILY. How long have you been working on it?
RICHARD. I don't have much time. (*Emily has picked her cup up, just moving it around, looking at it. Silence.*) You drink a lot of coffee.

EMILY. Can I read what you've written? I'll be honest. No false compliments. I take art too seriously for that.
RICHARD. It's different for you. Your relationships aren't permanent.
EMILY. It's all in your point of view.
BARBARA. (*She comes in, dressed for the meeting.*) I need the car keys.
RICHARD. What's the meeting?
BARBARA. Oh, I won't go into that.
RICHARD. You want the car? (*She nods.*) It needs gas. And have him check the oil.
BARBARA. (*To Emily.*) You see how suburban this marriage has become?
RICHARD. She belongs to a communist cell.
BARBARA. Was that a joke? (*To Emily.*) How long has it been? Since you visited my house?
EMILY. Six years.
BARBARA. I'm glad you're here.
EMILY. You were nice to ask me.
BARBARA. You're my sister.
EMILY. I told Richard about the pills.
BARBARA. Yes . . . Make yourselves at home.
RICHARD. (*As Barbara starts to leave.*) Just a minute. You asked me to go with you to the meeting, right? (*She nods.*) And I refused. Well, I've just decided what to confront you about. Your sister's staying here. You should be at home. If you don't stay home and skip the damn meeting, there'll be hell to pay between us. How about that?
BARBARA. What were you two talking about?
RICHARD. You don't consent to my terms?
BARBARA. (*Pause.*) Well, I don't have any choice.
RICHARD. Are you going to the meeting? (*Barbara looks at him. Then she leaves.*)
EMILY. (*After a moment.*) I wanted to be a ballet dancer once.
RICHARD. Well, if we're going to be on our own, let's do something terrific.
EMILY. You should go on writing, Richard. There aren't many people I find it possible to have faith in . . . But I don't know. I don't know you very well, but I do—I do have that kind of faith in you.

RICHARD. Thank you.
EMILY. Sometimes we don't appreciate our own gifts. You know what I mean?
RICHARD. (*After a moment.*) Why don't I make us a terrific lunch?
EMILY. Something complicated. And fattening.
RICHARD. What about quiche lorraine? Do you like it?
EMILY. I love it.
RICHARD. And a cold Gewürtztraminer. And then a salade niçoise. How does that sound?
EMILY. Sinful.
RICHARD. Fresh strawberries and heavy cream for dessert. (*Pause. They look at one another.*)
EMILY. Well— (*He kisses her. She pulls back, then responds, kissing him, hard.*)

Scene 2. LUNCH

It's after lunch. The dishes have been cleared away. Emily and Richard are sitting over the last of the wine. There is hot coffee and brandy glasses. A bottle of brandy, about a third empty, is also on the table. For a little bit there is silence. Then Emily tips back her chair and giggles. She is still wearing her bathrobe. Richard looks at her; he smiles. She only laughs harder.

EMILY. Suddenly, I'm so happy!
RICHARD. Good.
EMILY. Deeply, sincerely happy! Tranquil. Content with the world. Reconciled to my existential predicament . . . Do you understand me?
RICHARD. I'd better clean all this up.
EMILY. No. Please. Don't retreat. Let's have another glass of wine . . I got a chill just then, a slight one, when you began to close yourself off from me, Dick.
RICHARD. (*Laughs. Pours more wine.*) We're behaving like a couple of drunks, Em.
EMILY. My analyst says drink is good for me. I use it like an encounter session . . . I don't know what he means by that.

RICHARD. I went to a shrink for four years. It cost me twenty thousand dollars.
EMILY. (*Touching Richard.*) We have to talk seriously, get it all in before *she* comes home.
RICHARD. (*Responding to her touch with a touch.*) Who's she? The cat's mother? (*He laughs.*)
EMILY. My mother always used to say that.
RICHARD. So did mine.
EMILY. Then it's a significant point of contact. (*She touches Richard again.*) Dick, maybe I am drunk.
RICHARD. Have a little more quiche.
EMILY. Such a good lunch. You're a marvelous cook. That's a part of it, too, I suppose.
RICHARD. What the hell are you talking about?
EMILY. You want to be a writer? Right? That's oral-anal, definitely. I can vouch for that. And you work on taxes. And you like to cook. Get it?
RICHARD. I don't handle money . . . I figure out ways to hold on to it.
EMILY. You're concerned with building it up, with protecting it . . . Do you have a b-m every day?
RICHARD. I'm fine.
EMILY. You don't eat properly.
RICHARD. You're company.
EMILY. You're sexy.
RICHARD. (*Smug.*) Not depressed now, are you?
EMILY. When is my sister coming back?
RICHARD. She didn't say.
EMILY. You know I'm not drunk. Just frightened. Of you and me. (*She goes to him, tenderly bites his ear.*) Do we have time?
RICHARD. You're sure you're not drunk?
EMILY. No. I just—I have to act on my beliefs, that's all. I do believe in you. I find you sincere.
RICHARD. If a little bit constipated.
EMILY. Writers are, you know. Oral-anal. That's why I'm so attracted to the type I guess. I'm not a good writer. Barbara was right. But I want—I want to have a baby, or sex, or something with a genius.
RICHARD. Oh, well, I'm no genius.
EMILY. How do you know? You've led such a repressed life . . .

If I were honest, really honest, I'd dream about Norman Mailer—I mean as a sex symbol. He's repulsive, but he is the most fantastic writer. And I think you could be that kind of a writer.
RICHARD. I don't know that many dirty words.
EMILY. You've built up so many defenses. I can see it. Even in your muscles. The way you hold your shoulders. You're so tense. I'd like to help you find some way to release all that vitality. (*He looks at her, and pours them both more brandy.*)
RICHARD. You want to go to bed?
EMILY. After I read the play . . . No. You sit and read it to me. I'll be very quiet.
RICHARD. No. I'm too drunk.
EMILY. We can have coffee first.
RICHARD. Listen, Barbara could be back any minute.
EMILY. I like that. You're embarrassed.
RICHARD. You shouldn't denigrate yourself, you know that. I bet you're a terrific writer.
EMILY. You've never read anything of mine, have you? (*Richard shakes his head no.*) That's good. It makes things—virginal between us . . . I'm thirty-eight years old. I've been writing since college. I've been interviewed on tv; they may even offer me my own show. But I'm bored.
RICHARD. Me, too. I'm very bored.
EMILY. We're alike, aren't we. Both of us hurt by life. We're damaged people, Richard.
RICHARD. The truth is, Emily, that I'm more damaged than you are.
EMILY. Oh, I don't think so.
RICHARD. Yes I am. I'm practically the most damaged person I know.
EMILY. You see—now you're denigrating yourself. We're so much alike.
RICHARD. Maybe you're right. You could be more damaged. (*He touches her back.*)
EMILY. I'm so fed up with ambivalence . . . Let's screw.
RICHARD. (*After a moment.*) That's very interesting. I've just realized how sexually exciting it is to hear intercourse referred to colloquially.
EMILY. (*She is enjoying the massage that Richard has been giving her.*) I'm going to have to go back into group again. I can

feel it building up. I think I need a primal—I taught myself. The pain's building up. I'm descending into unreality. (*Richard stops massaging her, turns her to kiss her.*) I don't mean I'm going crazy. Have you ever tried it? (*He kisses her, she pulls back a little, kisses the hand he has on her upper arm.*)
RICHARD. I don't know much about psychology. Even after my shrink.
EMILY. Go on—your hands feel wonderful. The whole point of primal therapy is—various things happened when we were little. Things that make reality unbearable. So we become unreal. Just in order to cope with the world . . . You reach back into your childhood, and find the primal experience and release it. When you get there, you know it, because of the scream. It's—ear shattering. (*She caresses him, begins to unbutton his shirt.*) You should try it. Sexually it changed my whole life. I mean, I had no idea what an orgasm was until I had my first primal. (*They kiss.*) Men need it, too. We all use sex as a tool of unreality. (*Richard is out of his shirt now. He is undoing Emily's robe.*) Would you like to try for a primal?
RICHARD. Why not?
EMILY. (*Hesitating herself about this seduction.*) Are you afraid?
RICHARD. No.
EMILY. Maybe you'd rather wait until Barbara's here.
RICHARD. What do I do? (*A pause. They look at one another. They kiss again.*) Before we begin, I want to be honest. I feel this need to be completely honest with you. Do you understand, Emily?
EMILY. I think so.
RICHARD. There's no play. I haven't even started to write it. I just—talk about it. It's something I'd like to do sometime.
EMILY. I see.
RICHARD. See. You're angry.
EMILY. No I'm not. I'm just disappointed. Excuse me. (*Pause. She gets on the floor, goes into a tantrum like a child. She is very serious about it.*) I'll kill you, Daddy. You promised. I hate you. Daddy. Daddy. Daddy. (*And she achieves her version of the primal scream. Emily cries, and sits up.*) All right. I can cope with it.
RICHARD. I'm sorry.
EMILY. Do you believe me now? Do you see what a primal

scream can do for you? (*Richard shrugs.*) What's so hard about an act of faith? Give it a try.
RICHARD. I don't know.
EMILY. You don't know much about anything do you?
RICHARD. Don't you start on me. You're not even my wife.
EMILY. Sister-in-law. Why don't you take the damn robe off me? Or get me into the bedroom. Or on the floor. I've given you every opportunity I could. You're just humiliating me.
RICHARD. Wait a minute. We're in the kitchen. She could be walking in the door at any minute . . . I'll try. What do I do?
EMILY. The first thing is to relax. That's important. And just start talking. About your childhood. About what it was like.
RICHARD. Just at random?
EMILY. That's right. (*Pause.*)
RICHARD. I guess I don't know where to begin.
EMILY. Anywhere . . . What about a birthday, or Christmas. A lot comes out about holidays.
RICHARD. Well, when I was six, I was supposed to have a birthday party. My first one. I remember my mother took me downtown and bought me a new suit for it, and new shoes. (*He rubs his neck.*) I'm getting a pain in my throat.
EMILY. That's good. That's the primal pain showing itself. Go on.
RICHARD. Mommy! Mommy! (*Richard and Emily are so engaged in their involvement with the primal that they have not heard Barbara come in from the garage. She has come in in time to hear his "Mommy! Mommy!" She gives them just another moment.*)
BARBARA. Good afternoon . . . It looks like you've been having an interesting day.
RICHARD. Hi . . . What time is it, anyway?
EMILY. Dick was interested in primal screams. I showed him what they are. He was just about to have his first primal. I could feel it coming.
BARBARA. You could feel it coming? His first primal scream?
EMILY. Have I said something wrong?
RICHARD. We're just a little drunk, that's all.
EMILY. It's wonderful how susceptible Richard is to new alternatives.
RICHARD. How was the meeting?
BARBARA. Go and get cleaned up. (*Richard gets off the floor.*)
EMILY. He's not a child.

BARBARA. Are you sure?
RICHARD. Now wait a minute—
BARBARA. And besides. This is none of your business. If he's going to learn primal screams, I'll teach them to him.
EMILY. If you only knew how.
BARBARA. What is it you know, Emily?
EMILY. Oh— (*She could say so much, but chooses to spare her sister.*) things . . . People find me quite perceptive.
BARBARA. I've been married to Dick for ten years now. I know—
EMILY. (*Cutting her off.*) Maybe the facts. But interpretations?
RICHARD. (*To Barbara.*) Did you have lunch?
BARBARA. Dick, please let us talk.
EMILY. He's rejected. That's the primal he would have gone into.
BARBARA. Please. I don't want to argue. It makes me sick to my stomach.
EMILY. I'd like to get to the bottom of that.
BARBARA. Have you come to an opinion? What am I? Sadomasochistic with compulsive overtones? Dementia praecox? You make me sick. You're my sister. But this is the first time you've been here in years.
EMILY. First time I was invited in years.
BARBARA. Do you call me on the phone? Do you write me? How do you expect me to trace you from one affair to the other? I never know what name the phone's listed under.
EMILY. Let's just clean the kitchen up.
BARBARA. Well? What's your answer? You called me all right. So I'd get involved in the mess and stop you from that imaginary suicide. I knew you weren't serious. How could you be?
EMILY. I was so serious.
BARBARA. I doubt it greatly.
RICHARD. Listen—
BARBARA. I'll call you when supper's ready.
EMILY. If you didn't think I was serious why did you tell me all that on the phone? About how you needed me? About how you need—
BARBARA. Shut up! I said that in a moment of stress.
RICHARD. What?
EMILY. Oh, she told me a lot about you and your marriage. I had an earful.
BARBARA. Why don't the two of you go out into the yard and

have a nice primal scream together. I'd like to have a quiet cup of tea. By myself. (*Richard shrugs. He is about to go.*) Oh, Dick. Something else. So Emily won't feel her weekend here's been wasted. (*He stops, looks at her. She smiles at him, as if the anger were over.*) I want a divorce.

Scene 3. DINNER

Nothing has been cleaned up. Added to the debris of lunch are some paper plates, a few opened cans, two empty beer bottles. Barbara and Richard sit, staring at one another.

BARBARA. Can I get you anything?
RICHARD. You're not my servant.
BARBARA. Am I being cruel? I don't want to be. (*Emily comes in, fully dressed—rather formally, dress, heels, etc.*)
EMILY. Hi. I thought maybe I could treat you two to dinner. How about it?
BARBARA. No, thanks.
EMILY. I can't help but feel guilty about this.
RICHARD. You didn't affect anything.
EMILY. Oh, I think I did.
BARBARA. Maybe we'd better cancel the rest of the weekend.
EMILY. I don't think you two should be alone.
RICHARD. Maybe I should pack up. I suppose you should stay on here.
BARBARA. Aren't you angry? Have we been lobotomized?
EMILY. Shock. It'll come, the thunderstorm of rage and rejection.
BARBARA. Emily, I know you'd like to help us, but you haven't so far. Have you?
EMILY. Because you lack commitment. You don't want to believe.
BARBARA. We're not talking about the same thing.
RICHARD. Have you had any affairs? Since we were married.
BARBARA. I asked you that this morning.
RICHARD. Did you?
BARBARA. In about five minutes I'll go up and pack and leave . . . Unless something stops me . . . Just tell me one thing. Do you believe I exist?

RICHARD. I think I'm going to throw up. (*He is sick. He exits. Physically, not referring to the conversation.*)
BARBARA. What did you do when Stevenson died?
EMILY. Who?
BARBARA. Adlai E. Stevenson.
EMILY. Do you think you should help him?
BARBARA. I locked myself into the bedroom— And I drank a whole bottle of Hennessey Three Star Brandy, in about fifteen minutes, and cried. I haven't cried since. Not about anything. That's odd.
EMILY. Politics have never been that important to me.
BARBARA. I know.
EMILY. Not that I'm frivolous.
BARBARA. The truth is Stevenson's death—killed my libido.
EMILY. Why? All of a sudden.
BARBARA. I don't know. I came in today. And I wasn't angry that he was being so childish with you. And I wasn't jealous. I mean—it was apparent—the two of you, if I'd been another hour or so later. I was just bored with it all. I'm bored with living. I've been overcome with accidie. (*Hesitation.*) Maybe if Stevenson were alive we would have had children.
RICHARD. (*He comes in, looking wan, still sick.*) I did throw up.
BARBARA. Why don't you take some milk?
RICHARD. No. Thanks.
BARBARA. Sit down.
RICHARD. Thanks.
EMILY. I think I'll change my clothes. (*She leaves. They look at one another.*)
BARBARA. I suppose we ought to talk about things.
RICHARD. I—don't think I can. It's hard—for me—to get the— I'm all constricted in my throat. Like—when I was a kid and cried. I feel like I might cry. I suppose I wasn't enough of a man for you. (*Barbara reaches out for him. Touches him tenderly.*) I'm not a very authoritative person.
BARBARA. Not many people are nowadays.
RICHARD. No.
BARBARA. There just—comes a time for endings.
RICHARD. I don't know that I could make it, living alone.
BARBARA. Why don't you quit the job. You've got money saved. I won't ask for alimony. You could try to write. Or—whatever—

RICHARD. I suppose I'll be mad as hell next week some time when it's too late. I'm always feeling things about a week too late.
BARBARA. At least you're feeling things.
RICHARD. I don't suppose you'd consider staying on for a while. Just to see what happens.
BARBARA. I don't think so, Dick.
RICHARD. Well—(*He is about to cry. He takes her in his arms. Kisses her, she doesn't resist.*) please, please. I'm a very dependent person. (*She rubs his hair, fondly.*) Oh, Jesus. I'm going to be sick again.
BARBARA. I'll stay the weekend. Emily and I both will. All right? (*Richard runs for the bathroom again. Emily comes in, in slacks now, and a sweater.*)
EMILY. I was giving you time alone.
BARBARA. We've finished.
EMILY. Literally? (*Barbara nods.*) I'm sorry.
BARBARA. I'm sorry you came into the middle of it all.
EMILY. I can't help but feel guilty. As if I started something. Just by being here.
BARBARA. Maybe you did. I doubt it.
EMILY. I'll get packed.
BARBARA. No. Stay the weekend. It'll be easier. I'll leave with you on Monday.
EMILY. Would you like to come to Washington? Stay in the apartment with me a while. I don't much want to be alone.
BARBARA. I don't think so.
EMILY. I feel so sorry for everybody. Me too . . . Last week, I'd just got home from the movies. It wasn't anything special. This woman—she's an editor of mine and I like her. And we decided to go to the Garbo revival and we saw *Ninotchka*. And I had a few drinks with her and came home. The apartment was dark, That congressman I'd been living with—well, he moved out; and I'm used to having a light left for me. I poured some scotch over ice, and then I didn't want it. And I ran a bath, but decided not to take it, so I got undressed and turned on the tv, and I stood there, flicking Dick Cavett off and on. So I got scared, and decided there had to be something I didn't feel ambivalent about. I got the pills down and put them into a pile and filled a glass with Tab. Well, for a long time, I couldn't make up my mind whether to take them or not. It was like—you remember when we used to

have that fan going all the time in the kitchen in summer? I'd look at the blades for a long time then and I'd want more than anything to stick my finger in and see whether the fan would stop or cut my finger off. I wonder about those things—
BARBARA. . . . Can you? Love?
EMILY. I love you.
BARBARA. That's easy. Love between sisters. We're programmed to love one another. But I mean—have you ever ached for someone? . . . You see, even when I talk about it it sounds stupid. But sometime in this time, I want to wake up convinced that I am not alone. That in the bed—or even five hundred miles away, there is another human being who really knows what I'm thinking. Do you read much biology?
EMILY. No. I don't read it at all. I don't like science.
BARBARA. Well, they've worked it out . . . How everyone says —my blue is different from your blue. How we don't know if any person sees the same color blue as any other one. I mean the sky is blue to me. Right now, a kind of—almost cobalt. And to you it could look like—what I call violet. And there can't be any peace in the world unless we all—see the same color blue. You know what I mean? Well, anyway, they've figured out now, that even if they could transplant my brain into your body for a while— hook it up to your eyes—I'd still see my blue. Because it's my brain that translates what the optic nerve sees. That was the most awful thing I ever read, I think. It made me feel—completely isolated. Because—it's not so much that you'll never see my blue as I'll never see yours. But that's romantic, too. Going crazy because brain transplants don't solve anything.
EMILY. Why don't you make us all some supper?
BARBARA. Bacon and eggs, and strong tea?
EMILY. That sounds good. And toast and butter.
BARBARA. I suppose he's still throwing up.
EMILY. He'll eat.
BARBARA. I know. Why don't you see how Dick is. I'd—rather not. (*Emily nods. She goes toward the bathroom.*)
EMILY. You seem so—coldblooded. Sometimes.
BARBARA. I'll scramble the eggs. With herbs. And there's some fresh parsley. Maybe even a bottle of white wine.
EMILY. If he's still sick, what should I do?
BARBARA. Hold his head. (*Emily leaves. Barbara goes to the refrigerator.*)

Property Plot

On *Stage:*

Scene 1

3 juice glasses
3 cups
3 saucers
3 small plates
3 spoons
3 knives
3 forks
Maple syrup bottle
Butter dish with butter
Bread
1 kitchen knife
Toaster
Cream pitcher with cream
Sugar bowl
Percolator or drip coffee pot
Kettle for water
Frying pan
6 oranges
Juice squeezer
Strainer
1 dish drainer with a few clean dishes in it
Dish cloth
Dish towel
Liquid soap
Mixing bowl
Spatula
Eggs
Carton of milk
1 box pancake mix
Sauce pan
1 daily New York *Times*
1 ball point pen
Whisk
Pancakes

Scene 2

Strike all breakfast dishes and paraphernalia
add:
2 wine glasses
1 empty wine bottle
1 wine bottle partially full
A few dirty dishes
Dish of fruit
Dish of cookies
Cheese platter with crackers and knife

Scene 3

Paper plates
1 can opener
Several empty food cans
2 empty beer cans
Personal props:
Cigars or cigarillos (Emily)
Lighter or matches (Emily and Richard)
Cigarettes (Emily and Richard)
Keys (Barbara)
Watch (Richard)

BITS AND PIECES

The first professional production of BITS AND PIECES was in New York City at The Manhattan Theatre Club, Lynne Meadow, Artistic Director, on November 5, 1974, with the following cast:

(in order of appearance)

PHILIP	David Snell
DOCTOR	James DeMarse
TECHNICIAN	Sloane Shelton
IRIS	Rochelle Oliver
HELEN	Chevi Colton
FARLEY	James DeMarse
MRS. EBERLY	Sloane Shelton
ANTONIO	James DeMarse
MONK	James DeMarse

Directed by Lynne Meadow
Modular scenic elements designed by Peter Larkin
Lighting designed by Arden Fingerhut
Costumes designed by Carol Oditz
Production Stage Manager—Richard Hoge

BITS AND PIECES

There are many scenes in this play, they happen in a number of places. Before each scene there is a title. The title should be shown to the audience by means of slide or projector. The scenery should be minimal. Most important is that the audience be helped in every way possible to understand when Iris is on her journey and when she has returned to the past life from which she started.

SCENE 1.   PHILIP AND THE PAST

Philip is alone on stage. He is holding a picture of an ancient Greek vase.

PHILIP. This vase was twenty-five hundred years old. It was made in Greece, when men knew gods and dark things moved beneath the earth. The painting on it has been evaluated in two ways. Some said it was the work of a master craftsman, one of the finest of the classical period. They pointed to the line of the shoulders, to the almost dancing movement of the figures . . . But others found the execution mediocre, the work of a hack. (*He puts the picture down, picks up a shard, a hunk of a vase.*) Unfortunately, while it was on loan to a museum, the vase broke. Only a few shards were left. The state of the art is no longer in question. It has become the work of a master craftsman. And time is standing still now, for the vase, for the man who painted it. And this piece—it's something to pick up in the night when you can't sleep and rub your hands around. A little powder talcums the fingers, and they've become 2,500 years old.

SCENE 2.   WHAT HAPPENS AFTER DEATH?

The Doctor and the Technician are working in a hospital "white room," adjacent to an operating room. They are surrounded by styrofoam boxes of various sizes. Each box is piled haphazardly on top of another. Each box contains one human organ; all the organs have been taken from Philip's body just after his death. He was a donor, and now his parts are packed up and being made ready for shipment. The Doctor and Technician have been working all day. They are tired. They have only a few more boxes to label and record.

DOCTOR. (*He is checking his records. He has lost track of one of the organs. He tries to get the attention of the Technician.*) Hey . . . Hey, did you see the liver anywhere?
TECHNICIAN. Under the kidney.
DOCTOR. No. It's not there.
TECHNICIAN. Really? I'm sure I put it there. Look again.
DOCTOR. I have looked. Twice. (*She comes over, finds it for for him.*) Thanks.
TECHNICIAN. When I label the eyes—the corneas—I mean, do I put left and right or what?
DOCTOR. Have you ever done this kind of work before?
TECHNICIAN. No. Usually they keep me down in obstetrics. I like it down there . . . So—do I put left and right, or what?
DOCTOR. It's optional . . . You know, this man—the guy who donated all this. He was incredible.
TECHNICIAN. All this stuff came from one body? (*The Doctor nods.*) Well, how many more organs do we have to label? . . . I'm hungry.
DOCTOR. You just ate a *Twinkie*.
TECHNICIAN. Well, we've been locked up in here working for hours and hours.
DOCTOR. There's never been one like this. I'm sure of it. He gave away everything. He—you know—he thought about it, and he made a will, and he arranged to have himself cut up and—distributed.
TECHNICIAN. If they're going to have many more like this, there's going to have to be some financial arrangement. I'm seventeen minutes into overtime.
DOCTOR. Listen . . . The thing is—suddenly—I have this irresistible urge to fuck you.
TECHNICIAN. Now? In the middle of all this?

30

DOCTOR. Why not?
TECHNICIAN. Forget it. His soul could be here right now. Floating all over his parts, trying to find a new host body. Please. Not here.
PHILIP. (*He comes on, speaks quite matter-of-factly.*) At least death was instantaneous. It took me completely by surprise. Even though I'd been lying there, waiting for it.

Scene 3. IRIS: THE MOURNING BEGINS

Iris and Helen are in the kitchen of what was Philip and Iris's apartment. Iris was his wife, Helen, his sister. The two women are sitting at the table. They both wear dark clothes. They have been at Philip's funeral. Now, after the people have gone, they are sitting and drinking.

IRIS. He was the most important person in my life. I lived for him. I thought about him all the time. We were attached to one another by a thin invisible unbreakable—thing. (*Helen looks at her. Short pause.*)
HELEN. Go ahead and cry. It would do you good.
IRIS. Would it? . . . We know he didn't give away the penis. He was very explicit about that.
HELEN. Would you like another drink?
IRIS. Why are you talking to me as if I'm retarded?
HELEN. Funerals are hard.
IRIS. David told me on the phone last night—he didn't want to come back for the funeral. It was no good he said, if his father wasn't going to be there. That's pretty good for a nine year old . . . I didn't feel much like being there either . . . There wasn't anything to bury. A little heap of unwanted stuff. The bones. There was nothing to do with the bones.
HELEN. Stop it, please.
IRIS. So, when the undertaker called, you know, to ask me what to do, I said we'll burn it, the remains. Just a few ashes in a little box, put into a bigger box and buried in the ground. . . . Did you know that ashes don't rot? He isn't even going to rot.
HELEN. Do you want me to leave, Iris?
IRIS. I will have another drink, thank you . . . I'm not a logical

person, Helen. That's why I can't figure it out. You and Philip were raised on syllogisms. I grew up with the collected poems of Robert and Elizabeth Browning.

HELEN. There's nothing difficult about logic.

IRIS. Oh. I think there is. There's a logic attached to all this death and dying. And I'm going to figure out what it is. I'm going to be the most logical of us all . . . For instance—more scotch, please. I don't think you put any scotch at all in my last drink. For instance, take how we got to the cemetery. There we were. Up the avenue, down the main street, onto the throughway. We were following the hearse. Until—did you notice when it was we weren't following the hearse any more? I didn't. But all at once it wasn't there. But I figured it out. The hearse takes a short cut. Or we take a long cut—and it gets to the cemetery ahead of us. And the whole thing is out and on display before the mourners turn up.

HELEN. You're being morbid.

IRIS. That bastard your brother didn't leave me anything to bury. How could he do that if he loved me? What am I going to do?

HELEN. You'd better go to bed.

IRIS. Don't you try to manage me!

HELEN. I'm trying to be sensible. Philip would want me to be sensible.

IRIS. Echo, echo—I've got to figure out what he was paying me back for. Giving himself away like that. Like pieces of a saint . . . Please. Get the hell out of here, will you? This is no time for sister-in-laws—sisters-in-law . . . Stay. I'm sorry. Let's have a drink together.

HELEN. You don't want me here.

IRIS. What do you want to do? Move in?

HELEN. Should I? For a few weeks?

IRIS. No.

HELEN. He was my brother.

IRIS. That's right.

HELEN. I'm very tired.

IRIS. I'm not going to live. I know it. I'm going to develop a wasting disease and die slowly.

HELEN. We'll talk about that later.

IRIS. I tried turning on the radiator in the living room. There wasn't any heat. I'm cold.

HELEN. Do you have any aspirin? Or something stronger. (*Iris does not respond. She has been drawn to Philip.*)
PHILIP. And save the Sunday *Times* till I've read it? . . . And don't use the business section for the garbage pail.
IRIS. I can't stand it when you're pompous.
PHILIP. You love me when I'm pompous. It makes me sexier.
IRIS. Go to hell.
PHILIP. Go to hell yourself.
IRIS. They don't have double beds in hell.
PHILIP. Then it must be heaven.
IRIS. (*Laughing.*) You bastard.
PHILIP. Sexy bastard. (*He leaves, Iris is back with Helen now.*)
IRIS. Let's stay up all night and talk about love, Helen.
HELEN. You need your sleep.
IRIS. I thought I'd sleep out there. On the sofa.
HELEN. You slept in the bed when he was in the hospital.
IRIS. It's different now.
HELEN. You can't have a nervous breakdown. You have obligations.
IRIS. He's dead. He's gone.
HELEN. I know that.
IRIS. Not like I know it.
HELEN. Let's not argue. I'm trying to help you. (*She takes out a list.*)
IRIS. Not now . . . Please. Put me to bed. Stay the night. Just one night more.
HELEN. You don't want me to move in here. You said so.
IRIS. Just as a guest.
HELEN. I have a home of my own. . . . You'll have to pack up the clothes. We should give them to the Salvation Army. It'll be a tax deduction. You can use it next year.
IRIS. Fine. You take care of it.
HELEN. No. You. And the books. You don't read French or German. You might as well give them away, too. Maybe to the university library. In his name . . . Oh, there's one—*A Child's Garden of Verses*. From when we were little. I'd like that, if you don't mind.
IRIS. All right. Go home. Leave me alone.
HELEN. Only a few more things. Did he leave a will?
IRIS. I'll kill myself. I'll jump out a window.

HELEN. Didn't he go over any of this with you?
IRIS. I won't be intimidated when I'm in mourning.
HELEN. Next week will be worse. You'll see.
IRIS. What's so important about the will? You want to know if you're a beneficiary? What shall we do, Helen? Make an agreement now, we'll split it all, fifty-fifty? My God, you want his, and mine, and the whole family's. Well. The money stops here. I'll be sure you don't get any of it.
HELEN. I thought you were going to kill yourself. (*Iris reaches out to hit Helen, who intercepts her fist and gets in a slap of her own. Iris stands a moment, dazed, and then cries.*)
IRIS. (*She sits down, talks really to herself.*) He never explained that I'd be all alone. Forever. He didn't go into that.
HELEN. I'm going to run a hot tub for you. Bubble bath. And then I'll bring you a hot drink. Tea with rum. And you'll drink it and fall asleep. Tomorrow you'll be thinking of other things.
IRIS. We really shouldn't argue.
HELEN. You'll put cream all over your body. Some good-smelling cream. You'll sleep. You'll see. (*She leaves, for the bathroom, to fix Iris's bath. Philip comes in with a book. He is the young Philip, in the early years of his teaching. Iris has gone to a mirror. She looks carefully at herself.*)
IRIS. Mirrors are absolutely fascinating. Look. There's something about the eyes. There's something strange about that woman's eyes. . . . Phil! Phil! I need you.
PHILIP. (*Now in the past with her.*) Come on! I just need five minutes more. I'll be there in five minutes.
IRIS. (*Directly to Philip.*) I was afraid. I looked in the mirror and I was afraid. There was something so odd—and I wanted to go on looking until I figured it out.
PHILIP. (*Into his book again.*) We'll talk about it at dinner.
IRIS. Dinner's been ready half an hour.
PHILIP. Heat it up.
IRIS. Why do you have to be such a damn scholar?
PHILIP. Because it's my business. To be a scholar.
IRIS. Well, you can think on your own time. Come eat your supper.
PHILIP. I'll be right there. I just want to finish this page.
IRIS. You just turned a page, you cheating bastard. You have sixty seconds to get to the table. If you don't, I'm picking up the phone

and calling Howard Garfield. He's been trying to seduce me for three weeks.
PHILIP. Howard Garfield's a prick. (*She leaves him for the kitchen.*)
IRIS. (*With her back to him.*) You haven't put the book down yet.
PHILIP. How do you know.
IRIS. I'm psychic. Twenty-seven seconds.
PHILIP. Are you at the phone?
IRIS. Come and see.
PHILIP. Howard Garfield? . . . Now I've forgotten why I was reading the damn dialogue.
IRIS. Then come eat your supper. You've got fifteen seconds.
PHILIP. Shit. Have your affair with the bastard then.
IRIS. Phil . . . Phil . . . (*She goes to him.*) I don't have a watch with a second hand.
PHILIP. (*He is angry. Then he finds it funny. He laughs.*) My God. Think what I'd be like if I had original ideas.
IRIS. Come on. It's roast beef. I got a special price today.
PHILIP. I like my work, but oh you kid. (*He pulls her down onto his lap.*)
IRIS. I love you despite your eccentricities.
PHILIP. Let's get married.
IRIS. Not again.
PHILIP. I want to marry you. I want to be the father of your children. Me Tarzan. You Jane.
IRIS. Why do you waste all that energy on books?
PHILIP. There's plenty for other things.
IRIS. I bet you're awful at touch football. The Kennedys are great at it.
PHILIP. They have more money than I do.
IRIS. Not much. I'll be very rich when we get married, won't I?
PHILIP. Very.
IRIS. That's good . . . I said I'd marry you.
PHILIP. I heard you.
IRIS. Good.
PHILIP. Good.
IRIS. I'm an idiot.
PHILIP. You'll be completely happy.
IRIS. Will I?
PHILIP. Now get the hell out of here and let me finish my work.

(*He dumps her on the floor and starts to make notes. Iris runs out, back to the apartment area.*)
IRIS. I hope the damn roast is burned to a crisp.
PHILIP. I like it that way. (*The Doctor is in the apartment area, sitting on the sofa. Iris hands him a drink.*)
IRIS. I'm a very rich widow, you know.
DOCTOR. So I've heard. Most donors are—upper middle or upper.
IRIS. I want the names of all the donees. For each organ you gave away.
DOCTOR. I'm afraid not.
IRIS. It isn't like adoption, Doctor. I'm not going to try to get the pieces back.
DOCTOR. It's a question of medical ethics.
IRIS. Doctor, my husband was unique—and while he was dying—the two months it took—he continued to be unusual. I have tapes he made for me. Points of view. Philosophical recollections. He thought they would last me as long as I needed. Keep us connected while I was grieving. They may. (*Iris takes out a cassette machine, puts in a cartridge, turns the machine on.*)
PHILIP. (*On the machine.*) What Osiris is, you see. He had a powerful magic. He gave the dead a drink of water, and that brought them back to life. Because the soul has to quench its thirst or die. (*Iris turns the tape off.*)
IRIS. All the tapes are like that. Not one personal remark. Not one intimate memory. When I've finished, I can donate them to a library.
DOCTOR. I was very moved by it.
IRIS. I have to have your list. It's—a kind of mission. It's crucial. He's dead. But his parts aren't. They aren't rotting away in the ground. They weren't burned to ashes. That was a present he gave me. Or a curse. He's somewhere, in someone's body. Alive, with blood running through him. Moving. A hand grasping some other woman's hand. And I could see that hand.
DOCTOR. All right. I'll do it. I'll try to get the list. If I fuck you. Right now. I have this thing, about making it with strangers.
IRIS. I always seem to bring out definitions in people . . . All right, Doctor, let's as you said, fuck. (*She abruptly begins to undress.*) I suppose you're blessed in your way. Hermes the messenger. I forget what the Egyptians called him.

PHILIP. Where the hell's my pipe? Did you hide it again? (*Iris turns when he calls her, then she turns back to the Doctor. Philip does not leave the room.*)
IRIS. (*To the Doctor.*) Don't worry, I'm not mad. Or if I am, it's harmless. A death psychosis. Gone in a month or two.
DOCTOR. Don't you have a bedroom? (*Iris leads him into the bedroom. As they are going out of the room, Philip comes down, takes the recorder, turns it on, speaks into it. He is making a recording for her.*)
PHILIP. I have it now. The clear, bright core. Here in my bed, waiting to die, I see the perfection of my essence. I see myself shining, phosphorescent in the darkness. Clear of mind, only functioning, heart beating, blood moving, fingers curling with my breath and moving out again, air coming in, sweat on my skin. This is what I am. The body living. And all there will be. Well, . . . The one breath that is left is frozen. Suspended. The heart contracted, about to beat. The diaphragm still stretched. The word not spoken. I would say something to her. She would say something. But, tranquil and quiet. The last second is about to flick by. The swelled artery stretched, bursts, and I am dead.

Scene 4.   THE JOURNEY BEGINS. IRIS IN CALIFORNIA

> *Iris has changed her clothes. It is a week or so later. She is with a young man, Farley. They are in Los Angeles, beside Farley's swimming pool. He is a plain but rather attractive person. Farley is paralyzed from the waist down and in a wheelchair, but although some of his movements are restricted, he is not a passive person. He speaks with an exaggeratedly British accent.*

IRIS. I don't know. I thought—just barging in. I had to see you.
FARLEY. My days are very free.
IRIS. (*She has been waiting for him to talk. The pause has become very difficult.*) I'm not supposed to be here. I bought your name and address. . . . I don't know how to— (*Another pause.*) Helen—my sister-in-law—thinks I'm crazy.
FARLEY. Do you want some tea? . . . I can make some . . . I don't really care for it.

IRIS. I thought you were English.
FARLEY. Canadian. . . . I came here to be in films. For God's sake, sit down. So he's in a variety of pieces, then—your husband.
IRIS. In a variety of places.
FARLEY. That must be unpleasant.
IRIS. Painful.
FARLEY. (*He is having her on.*) You loved him.
IRIS. Intensely.
FARLEY. Why the hell didn't you stay home in your nice little house and mourn, like a sensible widow?
IRIS. I couldn't . . . We were very close. Extremely close, Philip and I. And. I really can't stand it, you know, not having him. He gave his parts away for a reason. He wanted me to know something. I'm sure of it. I'm sure I'll have a sense of him again—when I see it. Whatever you have—or touch it—or—that's why I'm here
FARLEY. To find his little piece in me.
IRIS. I won't hurt you.
FARLEY. Do you know what piece I have, then?
IRIS. No. He just gave me a list.
FARLEY. Organ, organ, who's got the organ . . . I'm sorry.
IRIS. Please—won't you let me see it.
FARLEY. His eardrum? You must be joking.
IRIS. I don't make jokes.
FARLEY. They offered a leg first. It wasn't the first offer. But it has to be a pair of legs. It can't be just one, you see, it's got to be a matched set. But legs don't satisfy me. Not yet . . . But it was essential for me to hear. I needed his eardrum.
IRIS. Hear what?
FARLEY. You should be under guard.
IRIS. Look. I've got a light. Like the doctors use. It won't hurt. You'll turn to one side, and I'll put the light in your ear, and take a look. Just one look. (*She waits for a response.*) Do you want money?
FARLEY. Don't try to buy me! I don't need your money! I don't need anything from any of you . . . I collected a great deal for this. (*He means being crippled.*) I spend it, too. On books, and liquor, and clothes. I still like to wear good clothes.
IRIS. Please let me see it.
FARLEY. Suppose I showed you the wrong ear?

IRIS. I'd know.
FARLEY. Would you?
IRIS. Would you? (*That is, show the wrong ear.*)
FARLEY. You're absolutely bananas. (*He turns, Iris looks, then takes the light and puts it away.*)
PHILIP. (*Appearing as Iris looks in Farley's ear.*) How do you do. My name is Philip Uberman. I teach assorted subjects at various universities.
FARLEY. Is it all right?
IRIS. (*Happy at Philip's presence.*) Were you ever in a movie?
FARLEY. Three. I had no lines in the first two. They cut my scene out of the other one.
IRIS. I'm sorry.
FARLEY. I didn't want to be an actor—just to be in films. I thought it would make me handsome.
PHILIP. I'm a socialist. I inherited it from my father.
IRIS. I guess I'm an anarchist.
FARLEY. Really? I thought it was illegal.
IRIS. No. I'm the nonviolent kind.
PHILIP. There is no such thing as nonviolence.
FARLEY. I did it myself. I ran the bloody machine off the road. I was pissed. Just giving way to another cliche. Like the phony accent. . . . It's all right, being a cripple. It's less demanding.
IRIS. (*To Philip.*) Success is crucial to a man, isn't it?
FARLEY. (*Sensing her separateness.*) Is it all right? The ear? What did it look like? It feels odd, you know, someone else living in my head. (*Iris does not answer. A Mozart record is playing. It has grown louder as Farley talked, and Iris leaves him, moving to Philip.*)
PHILIP. We'll play music till dawn, and screw the neighbors.
IRIS. I love you.
PHILIP. Only because my book has been published today. And I will be a full professor and short of moral turpitude or other failing of character our future is secure.
IRIS. *Dionysius and the Moral Temper of the Athenians.* It'll be a best seller.
PHILIP. A first printing of two thousand.
IRIS. And it's so relevant.
PHILIP. Let's dance.
IRIS. To Mozart?

PHILIP. Why not.
IRIS. You're drunk.
PHILIP. Not much. Thanks for the champagne . . . Listen to this part. Right here. It's so damned personal.
IRIS. Mozart?
PHILIP. Why do you keep asking about Mozart?
IRIS. Okay. Let's dance . . . Let's toast the book. And the next one. And the next one.
PHILIP. Let's hope one of them's original.
IRIS. I'll just slip into something more comfortable, as the mummy said to the pharaoh. (*Philip groans.*)
PHILIP. Did you make that up?
IRIS. I've got a million of them.
PHILIP. Shut up and kiss me.
IRIS. Let's talk. All night. While the Mozart plays . . . Except at the good parts. Tell me about Ricardo's economic principles. Or the decline and fall of the Roman Empire. Anything. I just want to hear you talk.
PHILIP. Like a waterfall, babbling in the distance. Well, in the beginning, God made Karl Marx, and Karl Marx grew. On the first day, he went to God and said, here is my thesis. I've got to publish in order to become famous. On the second day, he went to God the Father and said: Only bullshit and cliches are written down. That's my antithesis.

Scene 5. A CONVERSATION BETWEEN TWO WOMEN

Iris and Helen are in Helen's apartment. They have had lunch, now, they are sitting, looking at Helen's photo albums, books, of clippings, etc. All of it, mementos of Philip. The two women are just getting to know one another. This is just after Philip and Iris were married.

HELEN. Don't ever tell him I showed it to you.
IRIS. (*Holding up a bronzed baby shoe.*) I think it's sweet.
HELEN. He'd kill me. He's forgotten about it, I'm sure.
IRIS. He was so little. Look at that little foot.
HELEN. Not so little. He must have been a year old. He didn't

walk till then. And he didn't talk until he was two. I was sure he was retarded. But once he started, he didn't shut up. Sentence after sentence. Talking on and on . . . He loved spaghetti, the canned spaghetti. But he couldn't say it. Pisgetti, he'd say. I'd say it to him, spa-get-ti. And he'd repeat it, spa-get-ti. Okay, spaghetti. Pisgetti. Our father loved to do it with him over and over. (*She laughs with the memory.*)

IRIS. Show me some more pictures.

HELEN. There aren't any more. You've seen everything.

IRIS. Tell me something else. Anything. Did you go to the movies together?

HELEN. A lot. When we saw *Hound of the Baskervilles*, we took turns looking at the screen. We were both scared.

IRIS. Tell me about when he was born.

HELEN. I don't remember that. I was so little myself.

IRIS. What did you do when they brought him home from the hospital? Was it sibling rivalry at first sight?

HELEN. He was so quiet. I remember that. He was boring. Sleeping all the time. Just laying there and grinning. He was too good natured to believe . . . Oh, and he liked beer. Dad used to give him little sips of beer.

IRIS. I love it. Go on. I want to pump you dry.

HELEN. . . . I had such a bad complexion when I was a girl. I ate too many starches.

IRIS. When he was in high school—was he a Romeo?

HELEN. . . . He's still my best friend. He always has been.

IRIS. I'm an only child . . .

HELEN. My first year in college. I was home over Christmas. And after breakfast, while I was still drinking my coffee, he called me on the phone. Where are you, I asked. We have to talk this way, he said. I can't tell you this face to face. What can't you tell me? What's so terrible? You tell me everything. I'm having a spiritual crisis, he said. I've become an atheist. So of course, I burst out laughing. God damn you, he said, and hung up on me. He never would talk to me about it after that. Not at all. Right now, I still don't know whether he's an atheist or not. You know, there are these subjects. He gets so stubborn. Nothing's going to move him from A to B. Nothing at all.

Scene 6. IRIS IN WISCONSIN

Mrs. Eberly's kitchen. There is an old, often-painted table, and three straight-backed chairs. Mrs. Eberly is shelling peas. Iris has just been let in to talk to her.

MRS. EBERLY. I have to go on workin' while we talk. I have my living to earn. You know how to shell peas? *(Iris nods.)* Show me. *(Iris takes a pea, shells it.)* You have to work faster than that.
IRIS. What do you do with them?
MRS. EBERLY. The shells or the peas? The shells I throw out. I don't keep pigs on my property. *(Pause. They work.)* And I don't have any sodas.
IRIS. I'm here because of my husband. He died recently.
MRS. EBERLY. People don't eat right. Not enough roughage.
IRIS. Your address was given to me by a doctor.
MRS. EBERLY. I don't do cures . . . If a doctor can't help you, I'm not going to try. I can tell by lookin' at you though. Your kidneys don't flush proper. Nobody pays attention to that anymore. My father had a glass of hot water with lemon in it every morning of his life. And he died of a stroke, not one of your dirty diseases like cancer. You don't believe me. You think, that's what they all say . . . Things used to be different. When I was a girl, I used to swim all the time. I was going to swim the English channel. First woman ever. I trained and trained. My father had me in the lake water soon as the ice thawed. I swam. For hours a day. The crawl, and the back stroke; my specialty was the butterfly. You know how that goes? Arms and legs together, then you push out. I was good. I had lots of power. And I was ready. My father was sure of it. And then that—bitch—that Gertrude Ederle got greased up and into the water 'fore we'd even left for England. So there was nothing left for me to do. Oh, for years I was a very unhappy person.
IRIS. I'm sorry.
MRS. EBERLY. You'll have to speak up. I don't hear good . . . I'm a medical phenomenon. But I suppose you know that. I was rotting away inside. So they cut it out and put in new stuff.
IRIS. That's what I've come the see you about.
MRS. EBERLY. Last month, God saved me. While I was on the operatin' table, when they were givin' me the ether, he came to

me in the form of Gabriel the archangel. And he said, "Gertrude, you will be saved. You will live and be fruitful." Since we was talkin' I asked him about my investments. "Should I buy or sell, God," I said. He paused a minute. Then he said, "Buy industrials and hold." . . . So I did . . . I put all my cash into stocks. Now I'm goin' to be rich. When I die, I'm leavin' the money back to God. He'll know what to do with it.
IRIS. My husband was your donor.
MRS. EBERLY. He gave me his lung? I trust in God. I take his advice. If more people listened to God, there'd be less divorce.
IRIS. I'm sorry, you're confusing me.
MRS. EBERLY. Oh, yes. That's what they all say . . . You want to see the scar? It's seventeen inches long. I charge, though. And then I invest the money. It's small investors like me that keep American business running. Did you know that?
IRIS. Yes. I want to see the scar. He'll come then. He won't leave me alone.
MRS. EBERLY. Jesus Christ the savior is always with us . . . Give me five dollars and I'll open up for you. *(Iris opens her purse, takes out five dollars and puts it onto the table. Mrs. Eberly picks it up, makes sure it's money, and opens her dress. The scar is huge, diagonal across her chest. It is suppurating and very ugly. Iris can't look at it.)* You have to kiss it. Because you could be Christ in disguise. There's no point in letting opportunity go by. If it turned out you were, I'd refund your money . . . All right, now. Kiss it, like a good girl. *(It takes a moment, but then Iris does kiss the scar.)* No. You aren't God. I thought not. *(Mrs. Eberly closes up the dress, buttons it up again. She is disappointed.)* You want your money back? No chance. You're a nice girl, though, you can live here with me if you want. I need someone to strain the fruit. My hands are stiffening up. You want the job?
PHILIP. *(Suddenly appearing.)* I don't feel like talking.
IRIS. Did I invent you?
MRS. EBERLY. *(Laughs.)* That all depends on how you look at it, don't it, dear. What's your name?
IRIS. Iris.
MRS. EBERLY. You ought to be married.
IRIS. My husband died.
MRS. EBERLY. Good for him. *(Philip has only passed through the stage. Now Mrs. Eberly leaves Iris alone. She hesitates, is lost*

without Philip. Then, she moves down to his chair as there is the sound of a key in the lock. Iris sits in the chair, afraid and angry. Philip walks into the light. It is eight years before he died. They have been married two years.)

IRIS. Phil? Phil? Is that you? . . . Who is it?

PHILIP. It's me. I still have my key . . . I hope I didn't frighten you.

IRIS. Give me the key.

PHILIP. Sure. *(He tosses the key down.)* I've got to get to school.

IRIS. What did you come for?

PHILIP. Books. I need some books.

IRIS. Do you want breakfast? I could make some eggs.

PHILIP. I don't like eggs.

IRIS. I've already eaten. *(Short pause. They look warily at one another.)*

PHILIP. Did you talk to your uncle?

IRIS. Did you see your cousin?

PHILIP. Not yet. I thought I'd let you go first.

IRIS. I've been busy.

PHILIP. Well, I'll come back next week for the rest of my clothes.

IRIS. I'd rather know in advance. So someone else can be here.

PHILIP. Anything you say.

IRIS. I'm trying to make a list. Of what we should each have.

PHILIP. You keep the china, all that stuff.

IRIS. And I suppose you want the *Britannica*?

PHILIP. That's right, Iris.

IRIS. Anything you say, Philip.

PHILIP. Philip?

IRIS. I don't have to call you Phil any more.

PHILIP. Most people do.

IRIS. Phil's a little boy's name. Now that you're getting a divorce, you're a big grown man.

PHILIP. *(He starts to leave.)* I'll have a lawyer call you in the morning.

IRIS. I'm sorry. I just get these trolls.

PHILIP. You sure as hell do.

IRIS. I had a migraine this morning when I woke up. About five

in the morning. It was all grey and ugly. There was soot on the window sill in the bedroom.
PHILIP. You should see a doctor.
IRIS. I'll call you Phil if you want.
PHILIP. What is this with names? You want me to call you I—I love you I, or give us a kiss, Ris?
IRIS. You made your point.
PHILIP. Damn it. Why did I come back here. I could have sent one of the grad students. Or had my secretary call.
IRIS. (*After a moment.*) There's no reason we can't be orderly about this.
PHILIP. Have you been sleeping all right?
IRIS. I'm going to apply to law school.
PHILIP. You look like you were up all night.
IRIS. The fact is, I want the *Britannica*, myself. I'll need it in school.
PHILIP. In law school?
IRIS. I may get my doctorate in English instead. I'm not sure.
PHILIP. Let's toss for it.
IRIS. You can buy another. (*Philip takes out a coin, tosses it.*) Tails.
PHILIP. Heads. You have any paper. I'll keep a list.
IRIS. Now the unabridged. (*He tosses again.*) Tails.
PHILIP. Heads again.
IRIS. You call the next one.
PHILIP. This is childish.
IRIS. Make it the Grote.
PHILIP. I don't want the Grote. You keep it.
IRIS. All right. You give me the dictionary and I'll take the Grote.
PHILIP. I *need* the dictionary.
IRIS. All right. I'll take the Grote and you take the bar glasses.
PHILIP. I don't want the fucking bar glasses . . . That's the whole thing. You manipulate me. From beginning to end. You're a fucking psychologist. That's what you are. (*He pounds his fist into the table.*)
IRIS. You wanted to beat me, didn't you?
PHILIP. All the time. And I should have. You needed it.
IRIS. Hit me now if it helps you.
PHILIP. No.
IRIS. Go ahead. Maybe then we can talk to one another.

PHILIP. Jesus. Manipulation.
IRIS. I'd like to indulge in an act of rage myself. I'd like to take my coffee cup and break it over your head. I'd like to scald you with boiling coffee, all over your face and in your eyes. And rip your clothes apart with my nails. I'd like to take the fucking bar glasses and shatter them and grind the fragments up and feed them to you with a sterling silver spoon, so you'd writhe on the floor with your intestines bleeding . . . I'm not ready to live alone. Not at all. (*Pause.*)
PHILIP. I'd better leave.
IRIS. (*Going on.*) I know. We're not good for one another. We just—it's chemical or something. We fight all the time. You were a fool for marrying me.
PHILIP. I'm a fool to put up with all this nonsense. Come on. Go wash your face and comb your hair. Do what I told you for Christ's sake or I'll start socking you around. (*She looks at him, leaves. He pauses, sits in his chair, lights out.*)

SCENE 7. ANOTHER CONVERSATION
BETWEEN TWO WOMEN

Iris's living room. She is with Helen. It is long before Philip's illness.

IRIS. I wish you'd stay. At least till Phil gets home . . . At least for some dinner.
HELEN. No. Thank you.
IRIS. Why just drop in for five minutes at a time, Helen? You could do that on the phone. You should stay with us. Spend time with us.
HELEN. I'm sorry.
IRIS. Have I done something? Are you angry with me?
HELEN. Well then, I'll be going.
IRIS. What's wrong, Helen?
HELEN. Nothing.
IRIS. You sit there and you stare at me. What're you trying to tell me?
HELEN. Philip told me you're going to have a baby.
IRIS. That's right.

HELEN. I'm glad.
IRIS. Good.
HELEN. When?
IRIS. About six months . . . nothing shows yet.
HELEN. (*Brightly.*) Do you want a boy or a girl?
IRIS. I don't care. Both . . . Maybe it'll be twins.
HELEN. It's a good thing you're not a career girl like me.
IRIS. Come on, hang around, Helen. We'll have a drink. Maybe some wine. I feel like celebrating . . . Maybe on Saturday we can go shopping, get started with the layette . . . I guess people still buy layettes. (*She laughs.*) I'm going to feel so odd, being a mother. (*She hugs Helen.*)
HELEN. I'm sure you'll adjust to it.
IRIS. We want you to be part of it—of everything—of—you know, what the hell.
HELEN. I know. (*She smiles.*)
IRIS. I like you, Helen.
HELEN. I know.
IRIS. Well? Don't you like me?
HELEN. Of course. Of course I do. You've been good for him, too. For Phil . . . And I'm certainly very happy you're going to have a baby. (*She reaches for a cup of coffee, spills it, starts to cry.*) Oh, damn it. Damn it!
IRIS. I'll get something to clean it up.
HELEN. Don't bother. I'm fine. I'm fine. I just—it's all over the floor. (*She gets Kleenex out of her purse, sops it up. Iris helps her. Both women are on the floor, they look at one another, then they laugh. Helen laughs even more than Iris.*)
IRIS. Hell, we'll regard it as a christening. An early christening. (*Pause. They look at each other. Iris gets a cigarette, lights it.*)
HELEN. You know, I'm a shy person.
IRIS. I know that.
HELEN. It's hard for me to express myself.
IRIS. I know that, Helen.
HELEN. Sometimes I would just like to lock my apartment, and double-lock it and never go back. I mean, just take a suitcase and never go back. I could go to—San Francisco, or Peoria, or Rio de Janeiro. I have no obligations. I could go anywhere, and I could be anything. I could go back to school.
IRIS. (*After a moment.*) So. Could you stay for supper?

HELEN. (*With a little laugh.*) Yes. I'd like that. I'd like to stay.
IRIS. Listen. I've got the vitamin pills, and the calcium pills, all that stuff . . . And I've got morning sickness. (*Helen has not been paying much attention.*) Would you rather talk about something else?
HELEN. Well—it's an area of experience I don't know anything about.
IRIS. For God's sake, nobody's a spinster any more!
HELEN. I have had a perfectly adequate sex life. And I'm not in love with my brother. And I'm just not interested in pregnancy, all right? I mean— (*She tries to make a joke.*) I mean, rabbits do it all the time. It's not such a big deal. (*Neither of them finds it funny.*) You know, Iris, some people just—I really don't want anyone to be my whole life. I really don't.
IRIS. Oh, God, you don't know what you're missing, Helen. I wake up in the morning and I *want* to take his grapefruit and cut it in half and cut up all the little segments very neatly. You know what I mean?
HELEN. It's just not for me . . . I've never met someone I could love wholeheartedly. I used to think there was something wrong with me. People were planning to devote their lives to one another right and left.
IRIS. I have this feeling that if we go on talking like this, it's going to hurt my baby, so will you please shut up, Helen . . . I'm sorry, they say women get very emotional. Well, I'm very emotional, and I want to have nothing but happiness around my baby. For the next six months, I don't plan to have an argument. Or to listen to one. (*Helen looks at her, holds out her arms, Iris goes to her, Helen hugs her, very maternally.*)
HELEN. You know, if it's a girl, I'd really like you to consider naming her after our mother.

Scene 8.   IRIS IN ROME

Iris has a piece of paper with her, a list on which the names of the donors and their addresses appear. She doesn't know how to find her way in this strange neighborhood. This is a slum, in the worst possible section of Rome. All around her is the sound of women shouting, children crying, cats yowling. A man, Antonio, is sitting on the steps of a tenement. He has a bottle of wine and is half drunk already. Iris walks hesitantly up to him. Antonio will only be able to speak in Italian. There should be subtitles to the scene.

IRIS. Prego. Signore Antonio Vivaldi . . . Where do I find him?
ANTONIO. (In Italian.) I'm Vivaldi, what do you want? (Sono Vivaldi. Cosa volete?)
IRIS. (Enunciating carefully.) I'm looking for Antonio Vivaldi. (She fishes in her purse for another piece of paper, looks at it, reads awkwardly from it in Italian.) I'm looking for Antonio Vivaldi.
ANTONIO. (In Italian.) Damn it. I *am* Vivaldi. (Porce Madonna. Son' io Vivaldi.)
IRIS. Do you speak English?
ANTONIO. (Simultaneously, in Italian.) Don't you speak Italian? (Non parlate Italiano, voi?)
IRIS. Antonio Vivaldi?
ANTONIO. (Pointing to himself.) That's me. You want to hire me? I've gone honest. (Ecco mi. Ma che cazzo voleta? Son onestu orami. Cazzo.)
IRIS. Oh. You're Vivaldi. . . . How do you do? Are you related to the composer? (Antonio stares at her. Iris starts to find her Italian phrase book.)
ANTONIO. Get the hell out of here, will you? I want to drink privately. (Ma va mori' ammasato, va. Hai capito? Non vedi che sto bevando?)
IRIS. The composer. Musica . . . Maestro. Maestro.
ANTONIO. (He is afraid, ready to run away.) Maestro? How'd you know they call me that? (Maestro? Maestro? Come sai che mi chiammaro cosi?)
IRIS. Don't be afraid. I just want to see—you had an operation. Hospital? . . . How do you say it? Hospitale? Dottore?
ANTONIO. You're sick? I was, too. Lousy doctors. (Sei malatta? Vatene! Disgraziati medici!)
IRIS. You had a transplant . . . An organ. Can I see it? (She points to her eyes.)
ANTONIO. (He makes the evil eye at her.) You're a witch? You want to curse me? What'd I ever do to you? (Ma sei una strega! Cosa vovi? Vuoi maledirmi?) (He gets up, she pushes him down.)

IRIS. I have to see it. You have to let me see it. I'll find it. I can tell by the scar. (*She starts examining his body, opening his shirt, looking for a clue to the organ. She is quite desperate and really hurting Antonio.*) I have to see it. I need him.
ANTONIO. Help! Help! (Aiuto! Aiuto!) (*Antonio tries to beat her off, but Iris is stronger. The fight turns serious. Iris starts to choke him. He breaks away, makes an obscene gesture.*) Crazy bitch! (Figlia d'una mignotta.)
IRIS. The hand! He got the hand! (*She makes a grab for it. Philip appears suddenly. Iris is distracted from Antonio.*) Phil?
PHILIP. (In Italian. *He will have subtitles to translate his lines, too.*) Leave me alone . . . Damn it. You've got to let me have some privacy. (Lasciarmi. Per l'amure di dio, ogni tanto devi lasciarme in pace.)
ANTONIO. Holy Jesus. There's a witch loose. (Porca miseria! Aiuto! Qui c'è una strega.) (*He runs off.*)
IRIS. I don't understand you. I can't speak Italian. I'm lonely, Phil.
PHILIP. You've never known when to stop. It's time to stop now, Iris. (Non hai mai saputo smettere, Iris. Adesso smetti.)
IRIS. How do I get back to the hotel? (*Philip leaves her. She looks around, truly frightened.*) Does anyone here speak English?

SCENE 9.   KNOWING HOW IT IS GOING TO GO
BUT GOING ON ANYWAY

Philip is in a hospital bed. There is a bouquet of flowers, candy, a couple of books. Iris is sitting in a chair very close to the bed. Helen is sitting in another chair, a little removed from the other two.

HELEN. (*To Philip.*) It's funny, isn't it? The last few days, I've never felt closer to you.
IRIS. Were you friends—when you were little?
HELEN. Sometimes. Sometimes we hated one another . . . When he was seven, he was all muscle. You know, one of those swaggering boys who play all day at getting dirty. He never read a book. I don't know when he changed. He always had a cut or a scab

from falling, or a black eye. Oh, God, he was aggressive. It was hell growing up his sister.
PHILIP. Was it really?
HELEN. When's your next meal?
PHILIP. What difference does it make?
IRIS. It's five thirty.
HELEN. I think I'll leave when they bring the tray in.
PHILIP. You can leave now. It's all right, Helen. You don't have to spend every day here.
HELEN. Oh. Well, I don't mind. Not at all. I have a vacation coming to me. And they won't take the rest of the time off without paying me. You'll see. I'm never out of the office with a cold or, you know, when my period comes, any of those things. I'm healthy as a horse, actually, so I never use up the sick leave anyway . . . I talk too much. (*She grinds to a slow halt.*)
IRIS. Yes.
HELEN. I always did. Especially when there's a chance to say the wrong thing. Remember when I got in that freight elevator at work and whistled Dixie all the way up to my floor. (*She laughs uneasily.*) And there was a black operator. Just when the—you know, the civil rights movement was starting up. And when I heard myself, I was so embarrassed. I didn't know what to do, so I kept on whistling Dixie. (*She laughs again.*)
PHILIP. There's something about death that makes people stupid.
HELEN. Stop it, Phil.
PHILIP. I'm dying, Helen.
HELEN. I don't like to hear about it.
PHILIP. Really, you know, it's none of your business.
IRIS. Why don't you go have an early dinner. That way you can have a visit with him while I'm eating.
HELEN. He's spiteful. There's no reason to be spiteful. (*She leaves.*)
IRIS. You are.
PHILIP. I've got a right to be.
IRIS. Maybe I'd better take a walk.
PHILIP. No. Please. I don't want to be alone. Not yet.
IRIS. (*She holds his hand.*) Can I get you anything?
PHILIP. No.
IRIS. How about the pillow. Does it need any fluffing up.
PHILIP. I'm fine.

IRIS. It's hard to talk to you.
PHILIP. The doctor—that psychiatrist—she says in a while I'll want to be alone. Now—
IRIS. You're afraid.
PHILIP. God damn it! I'm thirsty. Get me something to drink, will you? Some ginger ale. (*He turns away from her. She moves off, encounters the Doctor.*)
DOCTOR. I'm sorry. It simply isn't operable.
IRIS. I don't believe that. My husband's a strong man. He's perfectly healthy. And he's young.
DOCTOR. We'd do much damage getting to it, Mrs. Uberman.
IRIS. I don't care. Even if he's an invalid. You've got to—
DOCTOR. The aneurism is leaking now . . . You understand? . . . It's a bubble, like a balloon in his artery. And it's growing bigger. When it bursts, suddenly, without any warning, well, that'll be it.
PHILIP. Where the hell are you? I'm thirsty. (*Iris comes back to him.*) Didn't they have any ice?
IRIS. Someone's bringing it.
PHILIP. I want to talk to him when he comes on rounds today. I want you to find out what the news is. About it.
IRIS. You know there isn't any, Phil. He told us. There's no way to know. You just have to keep still. The stiller you are the better your chance is.
PHILIP. I moved just now. I tried to crank up the damned bed. Nothing happened.
IRIS. It could. You shouldn't do that. I'll ring for the nurse.
PHILIP. I didn't do any damage . . . You aren't even upset, are you.
IRIS. Of course I am. We've got to be calm. Both of us. Now try to relax.
PHILIP. I suppose the sooner I die the better off you'd be. It's expensive keeping me here.
IRIS. That sounds like Helen. (*She takes his hand again.*)
PHILIP. Put your head down, on the bed. Like you did before. (*She does. He strokes it again.*) How's the boy?
IRIS. Fine. He wants to come and visit . . . They still won't let me bring him in.
PHILIP. Maybe I'll make it till he's twelve. Only three more years.

IRIS. He's making you a steam engine. It's supposed to be finished next week.
PHILIP. That's fine.
IRIS. I've been trying to figure out a way that you could do some work.
PHILIP. On what?
IRIS. You've got so many unfinished things. I was going through the papers—do you mind? And I sorted them. There are three short articles that just need a little work. A book review. And the book.
PHILIP. The book's out. It's impossible. Too much. And all the research left.
IRIS. Couldn't I do some of that?
PHILIP. Don't sit up. Please.
IRIS. What's the matter?
PHILIP. Lock the door. There's a lock on it, isn't there?
IRIS. We can't. You know what the doctor said.
PHILIP. I want you.
IRIS. I know. (*They kiss.*)
PHILIP. Jesus.
IRIS. We have to settle for this.
PHILIP. I can't.
IRIS. Talk to me about it. Tell me about loving me.
PHILIP. I want you.
IRIS. You love me.
PHILIP. What'll you do? When—you know.
IRIS. I don't know.
PHILIP. You won't have to work.
IRIS. Maybe I will anyway.
PHILIP. You'll marry again.
IRIS. I don't know.
PHILIP. You will. You're too fucking sexy not to.
IRIS. Would you mind?
PHILIP. I'll be dead.
IRIS. I don't want to talk about it.
PHILIP. My golf clubs. I'd hate to see you give them away. Maybe the boy could use them when he's old enough.
IRIS. I wouldn't give them away.
PHILIP. Remember? I'm the only professor of the philosophy of literature to win the club's open. In its history,

IRIS. You're the only one who's entered.
PHILIP. It's still a distinction.
IRIS. I won't marry. If you don't want me to.
PHILIP. Don't make stupid promises.
IRIS. I keep thinking there must be something to say and I'm forgetting it. (*She kisses him again.*)
PHILIP. Listen. Lock the door. It doesn't matter. An hour more or less. Please.
IRIS. You're sure?
PHILIP. Come to bed, honey.
IRIS. (*She gets on the bed. They lie there for a moment.*) No. Be still.
PHILIP. Forget it.
IRIS. We can be careful . . . Come on. We do it my way.
PHILIP. Whoever would've thought it. That dying's an aphrodiasiac.

SCENE 10. ASSORTED INFORMATION

Iris and Philip each at a lectern with scripts.

IRIS. Part 1. The Meeting.
PHILIP. I was walking to work one morning.
IRIS. I was sitting in the library doing my research for a term paper.
PHILIP. And she came toward me, with an open umbrella. It wasn't raining.
IRIS. And he stumbled against the chair.
PHILIP. So I asked her why. I thought it was a joke. A sorority initiation or something.
IRIS. He apologized and asked me to have coffee. But I had a class to get to.
PHILIP. She invited me back to her apartment.
IRIS. We didn't see each other for a few weeks after that.
PHILIP. We went to bed that very night.
IRIS. I loved him then.
PHILIP. Part. 2. The Ninth Anniversary.
IRIS. You'll be late for school.
PHILIP. I just decided to retire from teaching.

IRIS. And stay in bed all day?
PHILIP. Stay in bed with you all day.
IRIS. Come home early tonight.
PHILIP. Can't. There's a department meeting.
IRIS. Okay . . . Call the dean and give him your notice. Part 3. Getting Acquainted.
PHILIP. I was a champion marbles player when I was seven.
IRIS. Did you ever play hi-lo? You know with the paddle and the rubber ball?
PHILIP. No. But I played ping pong.
IRIS. Gnip gnop.
PHILIP. Did you win at it?
IRIS. Only once.
PHILIP. Well, then. You were all A's in graduate school.
IRIS. Almost. I got a B in library science.
PHILIP. Part 4. Domestic.
IRIS. You never wash out the bathttub.
PHILIP. I like handkerchiefs not Kleenex.
IRIS. Please, no chicory in the coffee this week.
PHILIP. You'd better go on a diet.
IRIS. You'd better start jogging.
PHILIP. Where's my red tie?
IRIS. I threw it out. Wear the blue striped one.
PHILIP. We're out of toilet paper.
IRIS. Part 5. Phone calls . . . Philip?
PHILIP. Hurry up. I've got to get to my ten o'clock.
IRIS. I went to the doctor today.
PHILIP. What's wrong?
IRIS. He says I'm pregnant.
PHILIP. Are you sure?
IRIS. Well—the rabbit is.
PHILIP. Jesus.
IRIS. Are you glad?
PHILIP. How long?
IRIS. In June. That's six months.
PHILIP. I'll be on sabbatical.
IRIS. Are you glad?
PHILIP. Stunned. I think so. Listen . . .
IRIS. I can't. My dime's up.
PHILIP. I'll call you. What's the number?

IRIS. Just tell me.
PHILIP. Hello. Hello. (*He shrugs. Hangs up the phone. Then he picks it up again. Iris picks hers up.*)
IRIS. Hello?
PHILIP. I love you.
IRIS. I'm in labor.
PHILIP. My God. And I'm in London.
IRIS. They're coming every fifteen minutes. How did the paper go?
PHILIP. I'm going to write a book.
IRIS. What shall I call it?
PHILIP. If it's a boy, call him David.
IRIS. And if it's a girl?
PHILIP. You name it.
IRIS. Clara. After your mother.
PHILIP. Swell. Is it fifteen minutes yet?
IRIS. Not quite.
PHILIP. Is Helen there?
IRIS. I have to hang up now dear.
PHILIP. I'm catching the next plane back.
IRIS. Get some rest . . . Are you there?
PHILIP. Do you need anything?
IRIS. I can't hear you.
PHILIP. I can't hear you. (*He can't hear, hangs up.*)
IRIS. Oh, I want you here. I love you.
PHILIP. I love you.
IRIS. Hello. Operator. Operator, I've been disconnected.
PHILIP. Last section.
IRIS. Take an aspirin and come to bed.
PHILIP. You know, about swinging. I don't think I'd like it.
IRIS. Want to try it?
PHILIP. We could spend a few weeks with Masters and Johnson.
IRIS. There's no such thing as a vaginal orgasm.
PHILIP. Who cares?
IRIS. You're drunk.
PHILIP. I want—
IRIS. (*At the same time.*) I love—
PHILIP. Why do you put the nightgown on if you're only going to have to take it off?
IRIS. It's sexy.
PHILIP. Did you take the pill?

IRIS. What about vasectomy?
PHILIP. No more kids.
IRIS. I think I'm starting change of life.
PHILIP. They have hormones now.
IRIS. Postscript. Honeymoon.
PHILIP. If anything happens to me, I want you to get married again, you understand?
IRIS. I'll be long gone and you'll be living with a twenty year old model.
PHILIP. It's a statistical fact. Men die first.
IRIS. I made a will.
PHILIP. There's a will in the safe deposit box.
IRIS. You won't die. You wouldn't. I insist on it. I'm going first.
PHILIP. I couldn't live without you.
IRIS. I couldn't live without you.

SCENE 11. IRIS ON TOP OF THE WORLD

Iris has a pack on her back, and in the manner of Chinese theatre, she performs a stylized, spiral motion that will indicate that she is climbing a mountain. Philip stands to one side, watching her. As the climb goes on, Iris will grow more tired, there is less oxygen in the air.

PHILIP. There's nothing left but my heart.
IRIS. Nothing.
PHILIP. Has the trip been successful.
IRIS. No. Not yet . . . I'm still hoping, though.
PHILIP. You should rest.
IRIS. The connections are wearing thin. I'm climbing to the top of the world, Phil . . . I thought it would be otherwise.
PHILIP. I expected more from dying, and it's so simple. And I've gone away too quickly. Iris?
IRIS. It's getting cold. I'd better move on. (*Iris goes on in her endless spiral, the lights fading on her completely after a bit. Philip is alone, in his area. It is the moment of his death.*)

Scene 12. Iris in India

Iris is sitting with a basket of food and wine, she has been eating. A Monk comes in.

IRIS. Good afternoon. I wondered when I'd see someone.
MONK. You found the food though.
IRIS. You speak English?
MONK. Whatever tongue may be necessary.
IRIS. Am I taking someone's meal?
MONK. May I sit with you?
IRIS. I was cold on the way up, but I'm quite comfortable, now. I expect it's the sun through the clouds or something.
MONK. Do you plan to stay here?
IRIS. I was looking for something—someone.
MONK. We leave a meal out every day, for someone who may have come without food.
IRIS. Oh. You get a lot of visitors then?
MONK. No.
IRIS. Are there many people here? I don't see—you know, houses, stores. I didn't even see any farms.
MONK. The soil is not good for growing things.
IRIS. Are you in charge?
MONK. We live in—openings of the mountain. You wouldn't notice them.
IRIS. You don't answer my questions.
MONK. I'm sorry. Ask one.
IRIS. I was trying to find someone. My husband died.
MONK. Yes.
IRIS. And I've been traveling, trying to find him.
MONK. His pieces.
IRIS. Yes. All over. And. They said. His heart. Could anyone do an operation like that up here?
MONK. Operation?
IRIS. A transplant.
MONK. That isn't what we did.
IRIS. I thought there was a mistake.
MONK. No mistake, the heart came here . . . Have you tried some of the wine? It's very good. It's made from spring flowers. *(He reaches in the basket, takes out two glasses, pours the wine.)*

IRIS. Thank you. But I don't like wine.
MONK. Cheers.
IRIS. Were you educated in England?
MONK. No. I've never been down this mountain.
IRIS. This is good . . . The wine. May I have some more? (*He pours some.*) I'm sorry. I don't want to—intrude. Is this a religious community?
MONK. Yes.
IRIS. You're very handsome. (*Short pause.*) I come from Indiana. Originally. I've lived most of my life in New York. In the United States . . . Should I worry about a sunburn? So high up. This is going to be the last stop on my trip. Then I'm going home . . . When I was little, my father gave me a book, about a boy and a girl who travelled all over the world. They had lived on a farm, but they left the farm and they went to Paris, France, and London. They even went to China. And when they came back, all the little girl wanted to do was to go out to the barn to see if her baby calf had grown any. I thought travel was something else. I expected to turn into a new person in each country. But what I've found is, I keep staying more and more the same. And I'm middle-aged . . . I think I'll do what Philip did. Then we'd have a chance, you know. The girl who gets my liver could marry the boy who got his bone marrow. If I die soon enough. Then we'd have more children. It bothers me not to have had more babies.
MONK. You could stay here with me.
IRIS. Do you find me pretty?
MONK. No. But I like you.
IRIS. Was that an eagle? Do they fly this high? I'll have to stay the night, I guess. I'd never get down the mountain by dark. And I stay with you?
MONK. No birds fly up here. It's going to rain. (*He packs up the food that's left, the glasses, etc.*)
IRIS. What happened to Philip's heart? Who got it?
MONK. I did.
IRIS. You seem so healthy.
MONK. I am.
IRIS. You said there was no operation. Is it something new? Something—Eastern?
MONK. I ate it.

LAST SCENE. MORE CONVERSATIONS BETWEEN TWO WOMEN

Iris and Helen at Iris's kitchen table. Iris is wearing paint spotted blue jeans.

HELEN. I thought you wouldn't want to be alone all day.
IRIS. I needed the coffee. And I needed a break from the painting. I'm going to be stiff tomorrow.
HELEN. I noticed how healthy the plants were.
IRIS. David's coming home for a few days tonight. I wanted to get his room all ready . . . But I can't put a wet bookcase in there.
HELEN. It's his birthday today, Phil's birthday.
IRIS. I know.
HELEN. I just meant—well, I was surprised to find you painting things today.
IRIS. I thought about painting this table purple. Like eating on an eggplant.
HELEN. Can I take you both out to supper? Pizza. He likes pizza . . . I got the nicest letter from him last week.
IRIS. David likes you.
HELEN. He's just like his father.
IRIS. No. Not really. Not at all.
HELEN. Whatever you say.
IRIS. Oh, come on, Helen.
HELEN. I've enrolled at the New School. Biology. And I'm going to take some math. Statistics . . . Something I can really get involved in . . . I've always felt very connected to science.
IRIS. All right, Helen. Phil's dead. I'm sorry . . . Now I have to go on working.
HELEN. You used to say he was your whole life.
IRIS. He was . . . I mean I thought he was. At that last place. While I was on my trip, Helen. I discovered that I had to make up my mind. To go on, or to stop. Whatever. So today, I decided to paint a bookcase. That's what I'm going to do. Even on my husband's birthday.
HELEN. I have to go to school. (*Helen leaves the kitchen. She goes to another area. She is in a tight light. She picks up a phone. Iris picks up her phone.*)

IRIS. I just can't go on talking about Phil every time we see one another, Helen.
HELEN. Why not?
IRIS. Because there's no point in it.
HELEN. Ever since you came back, you've been different. Are you in love with someone?
IRIS. Not on the phone, Helen.
HELEN. I'm sorry. It's been worrying me.
IRIS. How's school?
HELEN. I had to stop. All those fluorescent lights. They gave me headaches. And I can't go to school during the daytime. I mean, I don't want to give up my job.
IRIS. All right, Helen. No more about Phil then.
HELEN. David's starting to look just like him. (*They hang up. Then Iris picks hers up, followed by Helen.*) Hello?
IRIS. What's all this about your giving a cocktail party?
HELEN. For the victims of the Spanish Civil War.
IRIS. That was 1937.
HELEN. Well, some of them are still alive.
IRIS. All right. I'll come.
HELEN. I've been learning how to crochet.
IRIS. Isn't that hard on the eyes?
HELEN. Do you want me to make you an afghan?
IRIS. If you want to.
HELEN. How's David?
IRIS. He wants to be an engineer.
HELEN. I don't know how to go on, Iris. Really. I don't. (*Helen comes back into the kitchen.*) I don't know why. I—no, I wasn't even drunk. And I went home with him.
IRIS. Did you enjoy it?
HELEN. Yes.
IRIS. Well?
HELEN. What about you?
IRIS. I like being alone. For a while.
HELEN. You'll end up making someone else your whole life.
IRIS. Not ever again, Helen. No one.
HELEN. Sometimes I wonder if I'm capable of love.
IRIS. I love you, Helen.
HELEN. I love David. I'm sure of that . . . And you. I love you . . . Lately, for the last few years, I'm always afraid.

IRIS. About going on? (*Helen nods.*) I am too.
HELEN. I'm forty years old.
IRIS. When I was in India, I was on top of a mountain. And—it's not that I saw God—almost the reverse. I had this sure sensation, as firm and as real as a string of beads; mortality. I finally believed in mortality. I finally believed in mortality. Phil's dead. I'm going to die some time. Even my son will. I find that reassuring. (*She hands Helen an envelope.*) Here.
HELEN. What is it?
IRIS. The list. Of all the people who got his organs. I think you should take the trip. I think you should quit your job and pack one small suitcase and take the trip . . . I'll take care of your aquarium . . . You'll find out. It's good. Going crazy. I'm really glad I did it. Everything. Even being crazy. And then he'll be dead. For both of us. He'll be dead for the rest of our lives.

Property Plot

Note: In the original production, all the properties—except a very few personal props—were on stage through the entire play and selected from a storage space by the actors before the particular scenes began (see the *Production Note*).

On Stage:
Books
1 research book, with pencil (Philip)
8 styrofoam boxes in various sizes
Mailing labels
Clipboard and ballpoint pen (Technician)
Scotch bottle
2 old fashioned glasses
Plastic "ice cubes"
2 forks
2 knives
2 spoons
2 coffee cups
2 saucers
Tape cassette machine (with batteries, to be used)
Wheelchair (Farley, not on stage until Farley scene)
Afghan (Farley)
Photo album
1 bronzed baby shoe
1 basket with green peas in it
Cigarettes
Picture of ancient Greek vase
Piece of broken vase
Matches
Cheap wine bottle, partially full of red wine (Antonio)
Intravenous connection (optional, see *production note*)
Flowers
Candy
Paperback books
2 lecterns (see *production note*)
2 scripts
Basket of food and home-made wine
2 wine glasses

Envelope with paper inside (Iris)
2 telephone receivers
Back pack (Iris)

Off Stage:
Champagne glass with liquid (Philip)
Newly published book (Philip)

Personal:

Philip: { Trench coat
Umbrella
25¢ or 50¢ piece
Keys
Briefcase with piece of vase and picture of vase

Iris: { Purse
Doctor's ear light (in purse)
Tissues (in purse)
$5 bill (in purse)
Purse
Folded list (in purse)
Italian phrase book

Technician: Lab coat
Doctor: Resident's white jacket or lab coat

Production Note

The set: The play happens in a series of places and back and forth in time. Iris is the pivot around which it revolves and, in effect, the world comes to her although she is traveling to various places. Because many of the scenes are fragmentary, it is best not to have a realistic stage set. The furniture can be minimal (a few chairs, a table, etc.) and can be moved all over the stage. In the original production no furniture at all was used—instead, a series of modules designed by Peter Larkin became chairs, tables, book cases, everything in fact. The director can choose to use the whole stage for each scene or to set up "real" areas for Iris's apartment with an open, fluid area for the trip.

But what is most important is that the properties all be real. People should eat real food, drink real wine, and so on. Nothing like this should be mimed. And the director is encouraged to add whatever additional properties he thinks will bring each particular environment even more deeply into focus.

The lighting: One of the prime ways to make the play move more fluidly is by the lights. Again, the short, staccato nature of the scenes should be reflected in abrupt light changes. If the scene titles are used, they can be put on slides and projected with a rear projector to always form the back wall of the set.

The scene titles: The play was originally conceived with scene titles that were shown to the audience either by slides, small drops, etc. But, if the director feels the titles are impeding the flow of the play, he or she should feel free to cancel them out. In performance, we found out that not even the Italian subtitles were necessary for the Antonio scene. The audience knows what's being said by the action they're watching.

The staging: Most of the scenes do not have, in the traditional sense, beginnings and endings. They happen abruptly in Iris's mind. This can be a part of the staging itself. One reason for having the props on stage is that the actors can, by selecting them, begin a new scene and end an old one without a lighting change. By all means avoid a series of blackouts, or fadeups and fadeouts. The director can use his own sense of the rhythms of the play and the shifting environments, creating the beginnings and ends of sections with Iris herself.

"Bits and Pieces" was conceived as one long rhythmical whole and the less it starts and stops within itself, the more involved the audience will be in Iris's trip.

The casting: If both "Breakfast, Lunch, and Dinner" and "Bits and

Pieces" are done in the same evening (and that is the way they were originally meant to be performed) as few actors as possible should be used. The echoes in the family relationships can be emphasized by using the same actress for Iris and Barbara; and the same actress should play Helen and Emily; the actor who plays Richard could play all the male parts except Philip in "Bits and Pieces"; and one other actress should play the other women in "Bits and Pieces," so, the two plays can be performed with 5 actors.

NEW PLAYS

★ **AS BEES IN HONEY DROWN by Douglas Carter Beane.** Winner of the John Gassner Playwriting Award. A hot young novelist finds the subject of his new screenplay in a New York socialite who leads him into the world of *Auntie Mame* and *Breakfast at Tiffany's*, before she takes him for a ride. "A delicious soufflé of a satire ... [an] extremely entertaining fable for an age that always chooses image over substance." –*The NY Times* "... A witty assessment of one of the most active and relentless industries in a consumer society ... the creation of 'hot' young things, which the media have learned to mass produce with efficiency and zeal." –*The NY Daily News* [3M, 3W, flexible casting] ISBN: 0-8222-1651-5

★ **STUPID KIDS by John C. Russell.** In rapid, highly stylized scenes, the story follows four high-school students as they make their way from first through eighth period and beyond, struggling with the fears, frustrations, and longings peculiar to youth. "In STUPID KIDS ... playwright John C. Russell gets the opera of adolescence to a T ... The stylized teenspeak of STUPID KIDS ... suggests that Mr. Russell may have hidden a tape recorder under a desk in study hall somewhere and then scoured the tapes for good quotations ... it is the kids' insular, ceaselessly churning world, a pre-adult world of Doritos and libidos, that the playwright seeks to lay bare." –*The NY Times* "STUPID KIDS [is] a sharp-edged ... whoosh of teen angst and conformity anguish. It is also very funny." –*NY Newsday* [2M, 2W] ISBN: 0-8222-1698-1

★ **COLLECTED STORIES by Donald Margulies.** From Obie Award-winner Donald Margulies comes a provocative analysis of a student-teacher relationship that turns sour when the protégé becomes a rival. "With his fine ear for detail, Margulies creates an authentic, insular world, and he gives equal weight to the opposing viewpoints of two formidable characters." –*The LA Times* "This is probably Margulies' best play to date ..." –*The NY Post* "... always fluid and lively, the play is thick with ideas, like a stock-pot of good stew." –*The Village Voice* [2W] ISBN: 0-8222-1640-X

★ **FREEDOMLAND by Amy Freed.** An overdue showdown between a son and his father sets off fireworks that illuminate the neurosis, rage and anxiety of one family – and of America at the turn of the millennium. "FREEDOMLAND's more obvious links are to *Buried Child* and *Bosoms and Neglect*. Freed, like Guare, is an inspired wordsmith with a gift for surreal touches in situations grounded in familiar and real territory." –*Curtain Up* [3M, 4W] ISBN: 0-8222-1719-8

★ **STOP KISS by Diana Son.** A poignant and funny play about the ways, both sudden and slow, that lives can change irrevocably. "There's so much that is vital and exciting about STOP KISS ... you want to embrace this young author and cheer her onto other works ... the writing on display here is funny and credible ... you also will be charmed by its heartfelt characters and up-to-the-minute humor." –*The NY Daily News* "... irresistibly exciting ... a sweet, sad, and enchantingly sincere play." –*The NY Times* [3M, 3W] ISBN: 0-8222-1731-7

★ **THREE DAYS OF RAIN by Richard Greenberg.** The sins of fathers and mothers make for a bittersweet elegy in this poignant and revealing drama. "... a work so perfectly judged it heralds the arrival of a major playwright ... Greenberg is extraordinary." –*The NY Daily News* "Greenberg's play is filled with graceful passages that are by turns melancholy, harrowing, and often, quite funny." –*Variety* [2M, 1W] ISBN: 0-8222-1676-0

★ **THE WEIR by Conor McPherson.** In a bar in rural Ireland, the local men swap spooky stories in an attempt to impress a young woman from Dublin who recently moved into a nearby "haunted" house. However, the tables are soon turned when she spins a yarn of her own. "You shed all sense of time at this beautiful and devious new play." –*The NY Times* "Sheer theatrical magic. I have rarely been so convinced that I have just seen a modern classic. Tremendous." –*The London Daily Telegraph* [4M, 1W] ISBN: 0-8222-1706-6

DRAMATISTS PLAY SERVICE, INC.
440 Park Avenue South, New York, NY 10016 212-683-8960 Fax 212-213-1539
postmaster@dramatists.com   www.dramatists.com

NEW PLAYS

★ **CLOSER by Patrick Marber.** Winner of the 1998 Olivier Award for Best Play and the 1999 New York Drama Critics Circle Award for Best Foreign Play. Four lives intertwine over the course of four and a half years in this densely plotted, stinging look at modern love and betrayal. "CLOSER is a sad, savvy, often funny play that casts a steely, unblinking gaze at the world of relationships and lets you come to your own conclusions ... CLOSER does not merely hold your attention; it burrows into you." *–New York Magazine* "A powerful, darkly funny play about the cosmic collision between the sun of love and the comet of desire." *–Newsweek Magazine* [2M, 2W] ISBN: 0-8222-1722-8

★ **THE MOST FABULOUS STORY EVER TOLD by Paul Rudnick.** A stage manager, headset and prompt book at hand, brings the house lights to half, then dark, and cues the creation of the world. Throughout the play, she's in control of everything. In other words, she's either God, or she thinks she is. "Line by line, Mr. Rudnick may be the funniest writer for the stage in the United States today ... One-liners, epigrams, withering put-downs and flashing repartee: These are the candles that Mr. Rudnick lights instead of cursing the darkness ... a testament to the virtues of laughing ... and in laughter, there is something like the memory of Eden." *–The NY Times* "Funny it is ... consistently, rapaciously, deliriously ... easily the funniest play in town." *–Variety* [4M, 5W] ISBN: 0-8222-1720-1

★ **A DOLL'S HOUSE by Henrik Ibsen, adapted by Frank McGuinness.** Winner of the 1997 Tony Award for Best Revival. "New, raw, gut-twisting and gripping. Easily the hottest drama this season." *–USA Today* "Bold, brilliant and alive." *–The Wall Street Journal* "A thunderclap of an evening that takes your breath away." *–Time Magazine* [4M, 4W, 2 boys] ISBN: 0-8222-1636-1

★ **THE HERBAL BED by Peter Whelan.** The play is based on actual events which occurred in Stratford-upon-Avon in the summer of 1613, when William Shakespeare's elder daughter was publicly accused of having a sexual liaison with a married neighbor and family friend. "In his probing new play, THE HERBAL BED ... Peter Whelan muses about a sidelong event in the life of Shakespeare's family and creates a finely textured tapestry of love and lies in the early 17th-century Stratford." *–The NY Times* "It is a first rate drama with interesting moral issues of truth and expediency." *–The NY Post* [5M, 3W] ISBN: 0-8222-1675-2

★ **SNAKEBIT by David Marshall Grant.** A study of modern friendship when put to the test. "... a rather smart and absorbing evening of water-cooler theater, the intimate sort of Off-Broadway experience that has you picking apart the recognizable characters long after the curtain calls." *– The NY Times* "Off-Broadway keeps on presenting us with compelling reasons for going to the theater. The latest is SNAKEBIT, David Marshall Grant's smart new comic drama about being thirtysomething and losing one's way in life." *–The NY Daily News* [3M, 1W] ISBN: 0-8222-1724-4

★ **A QUESTION OF MERCY by David Rabe.** The Obie Award-winning playwright probes the sensitive and controversial issue of doctor-assisted suicide in the age of AIDS in this poignant drama. "There are many devastating ironies in Mr. Rabe's beautifully considered, piercingly clear-eyed work ..." *–The NY Times* "With unsettling candor and disturbing insight, the play arouses pity and understanding of a troubling subject ... Rabe's provocative tale is an affirmation of dignity that rings clear and true." *–Variety* [6M, 1W] ISBN: 0-8222-1643-4

★ **DIMLY PERCEIVED THREATS TO THE SYSTEM by Jon Klein.** Reality and fantasy overlap with hilarious results as this unforgettable family attempts to survive the nineties. "Here's a play whose point about fractured families goes to the heart, mind – and ears." *–The Washington Post* "... an end-of-the millennium comedy about a family on the verge of a nervous breakdown ... Trenchant and hilarious ..." *–The Baltimore Sun* [2M, 4W] ISBN: 0-8222-1677-9

DRAMATISTS PLAY SERVICE, INC.
440 Park Avenue South, New York, NY 10016 212-683-8960 Fax 212-213-1539
postmaster@dramatists.com   www.dramatists.com

NEW PLAYS

★ **HONOUR by Joanna Murray-Smith.** In a series of intense confrontations, a wife, husband, lover and daughter negotiate the forces of passion, history, responsibility and honour. "HONOUR makes for surprisingly interesting viewing. Tight, crackling dialogue (usually played out in punchy verbal duels) captures characters unable to deal with emotions ... Murray-Smith effectively places her characters in situations that strip away pretense." –*Variety* "... the play's virtues are strong: a distinctive theatrical voice, passionate concerns ... HONOUR might just capture a few honors of its own." –*Time Out Magazine* [1M, 3W] ISBN: 0-8222-1683-3

★ **MR. PETERS' CONNECTIONS by Arthur Miller.** Mr. Miller describes the protagonist as existing in a dream-like state when the mind is "freed to roam from real memories to conjectures, from trivialities to tragic insights, from terror of death to glorying in one's being alive." With this memory play, the Tony Award and Pulitzer Prize-winner reaffirms his stature as the world's foremost dramatist. "... a cross between Joycean stream-of-consciousness and Strindberg's dream plays, sweetened with a dose of William Saroyan's philosophical whimsy ... CONNECTIONS is most intriguing ..." –*The NY Times* [5M, 3W] ISBN: 0-8222-1687-6

★ **THE WAITING ROOM by Lisa Loomer.** Three women from different centuries meet in a doctor's waiting room in this dark comedy about the timeless quest for beauty – and its cost. "... THE WAITING ROOM ... is a bold, risky melange of conflicting elements that is ... terrifically moving ... There's no resisting the fierce emotional pull of the play." –*The NY Times* "... one of the high points of this year's Off-Broadway season ... THE WAITING ROOM is well worth a visit." –*Back Stage* [7M, 4W, flexible casting] ISBN: 0-8222-1594-2

★ **THE OLD SETTLER by John Henry Redwood.** A sweet-natured comedy about two church-going sisters in 1943 Harlem and the handsome young man who rents a room in their apartment. "For all of its decent sentiments, THE OLD SETTLER avoids sentimentality. It has the authenticity and lack of pretense of an Early American sampler." –*The NY Times* "We've had some fine plays Off-Broadway this season, and this is one of the best." –*The NY Post* [1M, 3W] ISBN: 0-8-222-1642-6

★ **LAST TRAIN TO NIBROC by Arlene Hutton.** In 1940 two young strangers share a seat on a train bound east only to find their paths will cross again. "All aboard. LAST TRAIN TO NIBROC is a sweetly told little chamber romance." –*Show Business* "... [a] gently charming little play, reminiscent of Thornton Wilder in its look at rustic Americans who are to be treasured for their simplicity and directness ..." –*Associated Press* "The old formula of boy wins girls, boy loses girl, boy wins girl still works ... [a] well-made play that perfectly captures a slice of small-town-life-gone-by." –*Back Stage* [1M, 1W] ISBN: 0-8222-1753-8

★ **OVER THE RIVER AND THROUGH THE WOODS by Joe DiPietro.** Nick sees both sets of his grandparents every Sunday for dinner. This is routine until he has to tell them that he's been offered a dream job in Seattle. The news doesn't sit so well. "A hilarious family comedy that is even funnier than his long running musical revue *I Love You, You're Perfect, Now Change*." –*Back Stage* "Loaded with laughs every step of the way." –*Star-Ledger* [3M, 3W] ISBN: 0-8222-1712-0

★ **SIDE MAN by Warren Leight.** 1999 Tony Award winner. This is the story of a broken family and the decline of jazz as popular entertainment. "... a tender, deeply personal memory play about the turmoil in the family of a jazz musician as his career crumbles at the dawn of the age of rock-and-roll ..." –*The NY Times* "[SIDE MAN] is an elegy for two things – a lost world and a lost love. When the two notes sound together in harmony, it is moving and graceful ..." –*The NY Daily News* "An atmospheric memory play...with crisp dialogue and clearly drawn characters ... reflects the passing of an era with persuasive insight ... The joy and despair of the musicians is skillfully illustrated." –*Variety* [5M, 3W] ISBN: 0-8222-1721-X

DRAMATISTS PLAY SERVICE, INC.
440 Park Avenue South, New York, NY 10016 212-683-8960 Fax 212-213-1539
postmaster@dramatists.com www.dramatists.com